Queen

The Life and Mission of Diana, Princess of Wales

By Michael W. Simmons

Copyright 2017 by Michael W. Simmons

Published by Make Profits Easy LLC

Profitsdaily123@aol.com

facebook.com/MakeProfitsEasy

Table of Contents

Introduction 4

Chapter One: The Honorable Diana Spencer ... 26

Chapter Two: Lady Diana Spencer 64

Chapter Three: Princess of Wales 109

Chapter Four: A Decade of Marriage 131

Chapter Five: The People's Princess 167

Further Reading 217

Introduction

"I always felt very different from everyone else, very detached. I knew I was going somewhere different but had no idea where. I said to my father when I was age 13, 'I know I'm going to marry someone in the public eye,' thinking more of being an ambassador's wife—not the top one."

Princess Diana, in an interview

During Princess Diana's lifetime, and especially since her death in 1997, her image has been shaped by the demands of the public that adored her. Since she first was identified as a potential royal bride in the early 1980s, tabloid journalists hounded her every step and tried to chronicle every moment of her life, however private and vulnerable. First labeled "Shy Di" when she was only a teenager, the story that people have been telling about Diana and her marriage to the Prince of

Wales in recent years is a story about a young woman who was in over her head from the very beginning, psychologically and emotionally worn down by her cheating husband and the incomprehensible attitudes of the royal family.

In part, this narrative has been created by the "semi-authorized" biography of Princess Diana written by Andrew Morton and published in 1992, which shed unprecedented light on the private lives of members of the royal family, particularly Diana herself. Its publication came as an enormous shock. For the first time, people learned that the Princess of Wales, the future Queen of England and the mother of two handsome little princes, had been aware since before her wedding that Prince Charles was in love with another woman, and had been carrying on an affair with her ever since. They learned that Diana's complete lack of preparation for the public role she was thrust into at age 19 resulted in her developing eating disorders and a host of self-harming behaviors. The result was a furious backlash in public opinion against the Prince of Wales, and a new image of Diana being formed in people's minds—that of a victim. She was no longer the fairy tale princess who had found her Prince Charming, but the fairy tale princess locked away in the high tower, longing for freedom.

Since the re-issue of Morton's landmark biography after Diana's death, with its shattering revelation that Diana had cooperated fully with its writing and provided the hours of taped interview material it was based on, a new picture of the "People's Princess" seems to have emerged between the lines. The Diana found in the published interview transcripts seems, if anything, more fragile than we ever thought her before. But those interviews also make plain the fact that Diana was much more than an unlucky teenage girl who happened to fall head over heels for an older man who thrust her into the limelight of royal existence and failed to support her afterwards. They show that she was more than a victim—she was a volunteer who deliberately sought the life of public service that only her position as Princess of Wales could make possible. Though it took her years to find her footing, and though she undoubtedly suffered a great deal during that process, she wasn't locked in any sort of tower. Rather, she chose the tower, day after day, until she began to regain her equilibrium. Once she had started to get her feet back underneath her, she opened that tower door herself and became a sort of princess errant—the self-styled "Queen of people's hearts"—a princess "for the world" and not just Britain.

Diana's interviews reveal that, even when she was a young girl, she had a certain sense that a great destiny lay in wait for her. Born to an old, storied, aristocratic English family, living her life half in the antiquated world of old family seats and historic heirlooms and half in the ordinary world where she worked as a ballet instructor and a kindergarten teacher, Diana was much more prepared for the royal role she would one day take up than most people realize. For evidence of this, we can look to Diana's recounting of the early days after she was first engaged to Prince Charles. Having been whisked away from a happy, even idyllic existence sharing a London house with several close girl friends from school, aware that she was about to marry a man who, even if he did love her, also loved someone else, Diana entertained profound doubts about the life she was about to embark upon. She had been chivvied into Clarence House, then the London residence of the Queen Mother, with no one to accompany her and little explanation as to what was about to happen to her. "It was like going into a hotel," she said:

"Everyone said: 'Why are you at Clarence House?'. I said I was told that I was expected to be at Clarence House. And I'd left my flat for the last time and suddenly I had a policeman. And my policeman, the night before the engagement, said to me: 'I just want you to know that this is your last night of freedom ever in the rest of your life, so make the most of it.' It was like a sword went in my heart. I thought, 'God,' then I sort of giggled like an immature girl."

This warning exacerbated her growing apprehensions about marrying a man whom she already suspected would never "look after her" in the way that she had hoped for, and as her misgivings grew, she became increasingly nostalgic for her old existence, and increasingly bewildered by the contrast between her old life as a kindergarten teacher and her new life as a representative of the royal family. But even if she felt like a fish out of water, she was, in fact, swimming:

"I missed my girls [her housemates] so much. I wanted to go back there and sit and giggle like we used to, and borrow clothes and chat about silly things, just being in my safe shell again. One day you've got the King and Queen of Sweden coming to give you their wedding present of four brass candlesticks, the next minute you get the President of Somewhere Else... I was just pushed into the fire, *but I have to say my upbringing was able to handle that.* It wasn't as though I was picked out like *My Fair Lady* and told to get on with it.

I did know how to react."

These words—"I did know how to react"—are the missing part of Diana's legend. Her extraordinary public outreach efforts in the final years of her life, championing the ill and the dying, promoting AIDS research, visiting battered women's shelters, and campaigning for an end to the use of landmines, were what led Prime Minister Tony Blair to dub Diana "the People's Princess" shortly after her death. But the idea that she was just a common girl plucked out of the masses and "told to get on with" the business of being a princess is erroneous. It is an idea that has gained traction, because the notion of the Princess being just a woman like everyone else helped her adoring public feel closer to her, and because the enormous sympathy that resulted for her after she allowed light to be shed on the miserable years of her marriage to Prince Charles naturally led to people depicting her as more vulnerable and hapless than she actually was.

But the truth was Diana had an upbringing that made her not at all an unlikely wife for the Prince of Wales, and it was a role that almost certainly would not have flattened her the way it did in the beginning if not for the fact that she was a teenage bride who was far too naïve to cope with being lied to by the older husband she adored. Diana was a born aristocrat, growing up a rambling English country farm that bordered the Queen's Sandringham estate residence, making her next-door neighbors with the royal family. She was playmates with the Queen's younger sons Prince Andrew and Prince Edward when she was a child, and Diana once remarked that she had never been over-awed by the prospect of having the Queen of England as a mother-in-law because she, Diana, had known her "since she was tiny". The Queen and Queen Mother had been godparents to members of Diana's family and attended their weddings. In other words, it was not unreasonable for Diana to believe that she could live happily as a member of the royal family—she had, after all, known them all her life. And her own family was sufficiently grand, in its way, that Diana had received a not insubstantial amount of training in the airs and graces expected of a princess.

The reasons why Diana floundered so badly in the early years of her marriage, before she began to develop the necessary assertiveness to address her husband's infidelity openly, were rooted in the instability of her own early family life. She was a child of divorce in a time and in a culture where divorce was practically unheard of, and the subsequent upheavals of being sent off to boarding school and having an overbearing stepmother to deal with created a deep-seated need for stability and honest, open affection between herself and those she was closest to. But this she did not receive during her marriage to Prince Charles. Over and over in her interviews, Diana refers to herself as "a virgin sacrifice" and "a lamb being led to the slaughter". By this, she meant that Charles, who at the age of 33 was under intense pressure from the Queen and the Duke of Edinburgh to settle down, marry, and produce an heir, had long ago realized that he would never be able to marry the woman he truly loved. Camilla Parker-Bowles was already married, and as the future head of the Church of England Charles was forbidden from marrying a divorced person. He had therefore decided to pick a girl he liked well enough, someone his family was sure to approve of, who would be willing to "do the job" of being Princess of Wales and later Queen of England, to provide him with children and attend public ceremonies. From the perspective of a royal prince, this was perhaps not such a strange attitude—after all, he came of a family which, for centuries, had been making marriages that had more to do with making alliances than with romance. But Diana, young as she was, did not understand this. It was hard for her not to be bowled over by the attentions of the man who was considered the most eligible bachelor in the world. But from the beginning, she sensed the "strange" quality of the attention he paid her, as she points out when she describes the afternoon Charles proposed to her:

"I went to Windsor and I arrived about 5 o'clock. He sat me down and said, 'I've missed you so much.' But there was never anything tactile about him. It was extraordinary, but I didn't have anything to go by because I had never had a boyfriend. I'd always kept them away, thought they were all trouble—and I couldn't handle it emotionally, I was very screwed up, I thought. Anyway, he said, 'Will you marry me?' and I laughed. I remember thinking, 'This is a joke,' and I said, 'Yeah, OK,' and laughed. He was deadly serious. He said, 'You do realize that one day you will be Queen.' And a voice said to me inside, 'You won't be Queen but you'll have a tough role.' So I thought 'OK', so I said yes. I said, 'I love you so much, I love you so much.' He said, 'Whatever love means.' He said it then. So I thought that was great! I thought he meant that! And so he ran upstairs and rang his mother.

"In my immaturity, which was enormous, I thought that he was very much in love with me... but it wasn't genuine. *For me it was like a call of duty, really—to go and work with the people.*"

Diana gave this account of Prince Charles's proposal and her decision to accept him with the benefit of more than a decade of hindsight and increasing maturity. She was, ten years after her wedding day, finally able to unravel her husband's emotions and motivations, which were so mysterious to her at the time. But what is made plain by her choice of words—"it was like a call of duty"—is that Diana was not some defenseless maiden snapped up by a rapacious prince. Diana's own sense of agency is often overlooked because it does not match the narrative of the ill-treated saint that people had taken so much to their hearts. She grasped what so many people fail to grasp about royal existence—that it is a life of public-facing duty which leaves little time for private indulgences. The fact that she always appeared smiling and composed in public, even when she had been sobbing in a car only moments before, or was on the verge of fainting from the malnutrition that resulted from her bulimia, is proof of that. Diana's remarkable moment of prescience—when she realized "you won't be Queen but you'll have a tough role"—did not arise from a feeling that she was incapable of the duty and sacrifice that being Queen would entail, but rather because she knew on some level that her husband would never change his ways. He would never be honest with her about his feelings for the woman who is now, in 2017, his wife, nor would he give her up. Diana sensed that the marriage he wanted, in which she shared his public life and provided him with heirs but never had the full measure of personal devotion that a wife expects from a husband, would be unsustainable in the long run. She married him anyway, because she loved him very much—but also because, in marrying him, she was stepping into a life of public service that would never end, even when the marriage inevitably disintegrated. Diana knew she would never be queen, but she knew she would be the mother of a future King, and as such would never be free of the ties of royal existence.

But this aspect of her marriage to Prince Charles was the one thing that did not alarm her. "For me it was like a call of duty," she said, "to go and work with the people." What the public did not know about Diana for many years, and what Prince Charles almost certainly did not know when he married her, was that she had felt a profound calling to live a life of service in one way or another since she was a small girl. Diana did not distinguish herself academically when she was at school—her three siblings were able scholars, but the distractions and upheavals of her home life made it difficult for Diana to concentrate on examinations and studying. But even as a schoolgirl, she distinguished herself by her acts of charity. Whether she was doing household chores and serving tea and biscuits to an elderly neighbor with dementia, or getting down on her hands and knees in order to connect with severely ill patients in a mental hospital, or dancing with the disabled at an asylum near her school, Diana proved early in life that she had a fearless compassion for people who were disregarded and pushed aside by society.

As Princess of Wales, she would make landmark speeches in the early days of the AIDS crisis, pleading with the public not to fear or despise persons affected by the virus, and to reach out to them in their suffering. She described her work with AIDS patients in the most moving terms, and her outreach towards them was all the more remarkable because AIDS was so little understood and so deeply stigmatized in the early

1990s. Back then, the fact that the Princess of Wales was willing to touch and embrace AIDS patients was nothing short of revolutionary. Diana describes how,

"…the AIDS hospice…was another stepping stone for me. I had always wanted to hug people in hospital beds. This particular man who was so ill started crying when I sat on his bed. He held my hand, and I thought, 'Diana, do it, just do it' and I gave him an enormous hug and it was just so touching because he clung to me and he cried…

"On the other side of the room, a very young man, who I can only describe as beautiful, lying in his bed, told me he was going to die about Christmas. And his lover, a man sitting in a chair, much older than him, was crying his eyes out, so I put my hand out to him and said: 'It's not supposed to be easy, all this. You've got a lot of anger in you, haven't you?' He said, 'Yes. Why him not me?' I said, 'Isn't it extraordinary, wherever I go, it's always those like you, sitting in a chair, who have to go through such hell, whereas those who accept they are going to die are calm?' He said, 'I didn't know that happened,' and I said, 'Well it does, you're not the only one. It's wonderful that you're actually by his bed. You'll learn so much from watching your friend.' He was crying his eyes out and clung on to my hand and I felt so comfortable in there. I just hated being taken away."

This kind of work was what Diana saw as the true purpose for her elevation to the role of Princess of Wales—and it was a purpose to which her husband was incidental. As unhappy as their broken marriage made her personally, she had not married him *only* for love—though she did love him, very much, for as long as he would let her. She had also married him so that she could do good in the world. Service and duties are bywords of royal existence, but in Diana's case, she had highly specific ideas about the sort of services she ought to perform and the specific needs she ought to fulfill, ideas that often clashed with the Palace's notion of how the Princess of Wales should perform her public duties. As she matured and discovered her own assertiveness, however, she increasingly struck out on these individualistic lines, and it was this which made her the most popular royal of modern times.

In Diana's interviews, she speaks candidly of the fact that Prince Charles was often jealous, especially in the early days of their marriage, of the fact that she had "stolen" his popularity. When their son Prince William was still a baby, Diana and Charles embarked on a six-week tour of Australia and New Zealand, where it seemed to strike Prince Charles for the first time that his wife was more beloved than he was:

> "Everybody always said when we were in the car, 'Oh, we're in the wrong side, we want to see her, we don't want to see him,' and that's all we could hear when we went down these crowds… Obviously he wasn't used to that, and nor was I. He took it out on me. He was jealous; I

understood the jealousy but I couldn't explain that I didn't ask for it. I kept saying, you've married someone, and whoever you'd have married would have been of interest, for the clothes, how she handles this, that, and the other... You build the building block for your wife to stand on... He didn't see that at all."

Yet again, as personally unhappy as Diana was made by the attitude which her husband chose to take up, she understood that she had a duty to the people who were responding to her with so much love and open-hearted affection. And again, her early training as the daughter of Earl Spencer, and the social graces she inherited from her mother, Frances Shand Kydd, served her in this role. Diana needed all of this preparation and training when she began to notice that it was not only her husband who saw her as a sort of pop star, reveling in her new-found status as a celebrity. The newspapers treated her as though she were a movie star, and to Diana, this was nothing short of a complete misapprehension of her character, and a distraction from the truly important work of her position. But she had no choice save to put on a composed smile and soldier through the barrage:

"I've got what my mother's got. However bloody you're feeling, you can put on the most amazing show of happiness. My mother is an expert at that. I've picked it up, kept the wolves from the door, but what I couldn't cope with in those dark ages was people saying, 'It's her fault' [meaning the tension in her marriage to Prince Charles.] I got that from everywhere, everywhere, the system, and the media started to say it was my fault—'I was the Marilyn Monroe of the 1980s and that I was adoring it.' I've never *ever* sat down and said: 'Hooray, how wonderful,' never, because the day I do that we're in trouble in this set-up. *I am performing a duty as the Princess of Wales as my time is allocated.* If life changes, it changes but at least when I finish, as I see it, my 12 to 15 years as Princess of Wales…I don't see it any longer, funnily enough."

Today, Diana's legend is so overshadowed by the tragedy of her death that it is sometimes difficult to remember that she was still a young woman when she died, just emerging into a new existence and a new strength. Liberated from her unhappy marriage at last, devoted to charity work, and determined to imbue her two sons with a set of values that would help them escape the social myopia that has so often characterized the royal family in recent times, Diana seemed poised at the time of her death to do very great things. We think of her death in terms of the loss she represented to the world. We do not, however, think deeply enough on the accomplishments she achieved in the years that were granted to her.

The fact that Diana was catapulted from her quiet, sober life as a 19-year old kindergarten teacher into being the most famous woman in the world, that she overcame eating disorders and intense emotional and psychological frailties dating from her early childhood in order to rise to her responsibilities and do all that was in her power to make life better for those she could help, is quite enough accomplishment to be going on with for one lifetime. Those who wish to honor Diana's legacy in this day and age would do well to remember that she was much more than a victim of an unhappy marriage or an out-of-touch monarchial institution—that she was a willing and conscientious volunteer for a life of public service. As she said in one of her interviews:

"I remember saying to myself: 'Right, Diana, it's no good, you've got to change it right round, this publicity, you've got to grow up and be responsible. You've got to understand that you can't do what other 26- and 27- year olds are doing. *You've been chosen to do a position so you must adapt to the position and stop fighting it*."

Diana will be remembered for many things—her suffering, beauty, style, compassion, motherhood, and outreach to the poor. But it should also be remembered that she was strong, that she adapted when she had to, and even, sometimes, made the world adapt to her. She was not a victim; she was a willing Princess. And she understood better than anyone what being a Princess truly meant.

Chapter One: The Honorable Diana Spencer

A Spencer childhood

The Honorable Diana Spencer was born on July 1, 1961. "The Honorable" is a curious and antiquated form of address, much more likely to make Americans think of a judge in a court of law than an infant girl. Though it is sometimes earned in service to the royal family, "Honorable" is most often a prefix which is awarded at birth to the children of viscounts and barons. It takes the place of other forms of address, such as "Miss" or "Mister", but only on paper and never in conversation. One would have been introduced to the young Diana as "Miss Diana Spencer"—"The Honorable Diana Spencer" was a usage reserved for correspondence and invitations. It was written on envelopes, or on place cards, but not used when speaking directly to her.

Diana was the fourth of five "Honorable" children born to her parents, the Viscount and Viscountess Althorp. With two older sisters preceding her, as well as a brother, John, who had been born with severe birth defects and lived for only ten hours after his birth, the Althorps had been hoping very much for a boy. Diana never seemed to escape the sense of disappointment that had attended her birth. The family had been counting so much on a boy's arrival that they had given no thoughts to names for a girl—she was ultimately called Diana for a famous Spencer ancestress, and Frances, for her mother. Diana's having been born a girl was hard on her mother, who felt enormously pressured to produce a son to carry on her husband's title, and the family tensions that erupted after Diana's birth were probably the ultimate cause of the failure of her parents' marriage. At the Spencers' insistence, Diana's mother—then a fiercely independent young woman of only twenty-three—was compelled to submit to a number of intrusive medical exams, as if the doctors would be able to determine what was wrong with her that she kept having one girl after another. It was a scene more appropriate to the 16th century court of Henry VIII than a modern aristocratic family in the sixties.

Even though Diana's parents produced a son three years later, Diana never quite escaped the sensation that she had disappointed and failed her family merely by existing. A few years before her death, she spoke to her biographer, Andrew Morton, regarding the troubles of her early childhood and their lingering effect in adulthood, and she pinpointed the disappointment over her sex as the beginning of many of her insecurities. "At the age of 14," she said, "I just remember thinking that I wasn't very good at anything, that I was hopeless. My brother was always the one getting exams at school and I was the dropout. I couldn't understand why I was perhaps a nuisance to have around... In later years, I've perceived [it] as being part of the son, the child who died before me... Both [parents] were crazy to have a son and heir, and there comes a third daughter. What a bore, we're going to have to try again."

When the longed-for boy appeared, the difference between his reception and Diana's reception could scarcely have been more marked. Diana was christened in Sandringham church, with family friends standing as godparents; her brother Charles was christened in Westminster Abbey, and the Queen herself was his first godparent. Though Diana has been presented in the media for years as a virtual commoner, an ordinary girl who was catapulted from rags to riches in marrying a prince, the Spencer family was in fact anything but common, save in the most literal sense of not being royal. The Spencers had accumulated a vast fortune in the 1400s, a fortune which had been considerably reduced by the time of Diana's birth five hundred years later, but they were by no means the cliché of the impoverished nobility, who acted as little more than stewards to their grand historical seats. Charles Spencer was born the heir to a coat of arms and family motto ("God defend the right"), and a family seat, Althorp House, which had been a gift to the family from King Charles II. The family also possessed a large collection of art and antiques which were worth considerable sums. While the Spencer family had never been among the first noble families in English history, they had survived the destructive fates of many grander and more ambitious clans by electing service to the monarchy, rather than vying to wrest power away from them. The Spencers possessed an earldom, and many members of their family had been ladies-in-waiting to Queens, or Lord Chamberlains and equerries to Kings. Both Diana's grandmothers, maternal and paternal, had been senior among the Queen Mother's personal attendants. This was the

Spencer legacy that only a son could rightfully claim as a birthright.

But for all Diana's anxieties about being a source of trouble to her family, she never resented her brother for having the greater claim to the illustrious Spencer legacy. Althorp House, which in Diana's childhood was still the seat of her grandfather, the seventh Earl, was rather terrifying to both Diana and her brother Charles when they were small. Like so many great historical houses, it seemed more like a museum of priceless touch-me-not antiquities than a place where children could make themselves at home. And the forbidding pall which hung over the house was not due solely to its age and air of majesty. Diana's grandfather, Earl Althorp, had a contentious and disapproving relationship with her father, the Viscount, known to his friends as Johnnie. Diana's father was too modern for her grandfather's tastes; the Earl was fiercely protective of Althorp House and the history it contained, and his tastes ran to art and music and literature. Johnnie Althorp was rather more in the playboy model of English aristocracy, and for most of Diana's childhood he was barely on speaking terms with his father.

Diana and her brother Charles were both rather overawed by their grandfather the Earl, but Diana enjoyed a very close relationship with her grandmother, the Countess, whom Diana referred to as "sweet, wonderful and very special. Divine really." Countess Spencer was well known for her charitable interests, and probably served as Diana's earliest inspiration for her interest in the plight of the ill and marginalized.

Diana grew up at Park Home in Nottingham, a place very unlike Althorp House. The lease to Park Home had been granted to Diana's grandfather by his friend, King George VI, and though it was large and gracious by the standards of most middle or lower class dwellings, with ten bedrooms, a swimming pool, a cricket pitch, garages, and a full complement of domestic staff, it seemed very cozy and normal to Diana and Charles when they were growing up. When their grandfather the Earl died in 1975, and the younger generation of Spencers took up residence in Althorp House full time, the children felt the loss of Park Home keenly. Charles Spencer later recalled going into each of the rooms and saying goodbye to them, as if they were each members of the family.

Notwithstanding the brooding atmosphere of emotional turmoil occasioned by their parents' crumbling marriage, the Spencer children's years at Park Home had been idyllic—rather like something from a storybook published before the turmoil and societal upheavals following the second World War. The wealth, privilege, and antiquity of the Spencer family ensured that the domestic life of the house ran along lines that had been set down for the proper upbringing of upper class children since the Victorian era. The children of Viscount Althorp grew up in their own private nursery, overseen by a nanny, and had lessons in their own schoolroom, overseen by a governess. Park House was equipped with spacious parklands full of game, and Diana was devoted to small animals—goldfish, hamsters, guinea pigs, rats, and cats, and as a child her cat Marmalade was notorious for refusing to tolerate the company of anyone save his mistress.

The manner in which Diana was brought up—nannies, governesses, visits to forbidding old houses stuffed with historical relics, lots of time in the fresh outdoor air of the countryside, horseback riding—marked her indelibly as the product of a dying way of aristocratic life. As her own brother remarked, "It was a privileged upbringing out of a different age, a distant way of living from your parents. I don't know anyone who brings up children like that anymore." There is good reason why the Spencers were among the last of their breed. Few aristocrats in Europe had survived both wars with their fortunes intact and their ancient family seats untouched by the bombing. Diana's upbringing would not have been in any way remarkable forty years earlier. In fact, she was raised in a manner that was remarkably similar to how the Queen and her sister Margaret had been brought up, before their uncle's abdication whisked the two young princesses away from their own idyllic country existence and into the hallowed halls of Buckingham Palace.

The greatest difference between Diana's upbringing and those of the royal princesses, at least before Elizabeth became heir to the throne, was the fact that the Queen had enjoyed a remarkably happy childhood and a very close relationship with her doting parents. Diana, by contrast, had all the accoutrements of a wealthy, aristocratic upbringing, but the Althorps, focused on their own domestic unhappiness, did not devote the same measure of care and attention towards their younger children that the Duke and Duchess of York had lavished on Princess Elizabeth and Princess Margaret. In both families, the children abided by a schedule of activities that ensured they led a nearly separate existence from their parents, save for brief, planned visits in the mornings and evenings—Charles Spencer was not permitted to take his suppers at the dinner table with his parents until he was seven years old. But while the Queen's parents had considered their time with their children to be the happiest part of their day, Diana's parents were more preoccupied by their personal troubles and less inclined to notice the insecurity and unhappiness of their younger children.

There is a poignant story told by Diana of her childhood, about the weight of disappointed expectations she carried with her at an early age.

She was preoccupied by burials and graveyards—not morbidly, but solemnly, as she buried her small pets who had died in tiny graves and fashioned tiny crosses for them out of sticks. Afterwards, she and Charles would often visit the nearby churchyard at Sandringham, where their brother John was buried. Both children would regard his grave somberly and wonder aloud how their lives might have been different had baby John lived. Diana was convinced that she never would have been born at all, since her parents would no longer have needed to try for a boy. Charles felt that her parents would have tried again for Diana, but that four children would have completed their family, and his own birth never would have occurred. It would seem to say much about the atmosphere hanging over both children's lives, that they could so easily and matter-of-factly envision a life which their parents would have preferred, a life in which neither of them had ever existed.

Privileged though they were, and similar though their upbringing was to that of aristocratic and even royal children a generation past, Diana's childhood was unlike that of her future mother-in-law in one significant way: she was not royal. This seems obvious enough, but it made all the difference to Diana's personality and the unhappy royal marriage that lay in her future. There were a number of superficial resemblances between the way Diana and her siblings were raised and the way in which other children in the upper echelons of British society were brought up, including royal children. But to be royal was to be set apart in a way that is difficult for anyone raised outside the system of the Palace and its courtiers to properly understand. When the Queen was in her early twenties, her governess, Marion Crawford, shocked the royal family by publishing an intimate memoir of her time with the royal family. After the book came out, the woman who had effectively raised the two princesses were instantly shut out of their lives forever, never again to receive a note or card from them, not even when she attempted suicide years later and died a broken, impoverished woman. Members of the royal family had it instilled in them from their earliest years that they were not like other people—perhaps not better, or worse than others, but different in a way that effectively seals them behind an impenetrable barrier for life. When Queen Elizabeth was a child, she socialized frequently with "suitable" children, the daughters of high ranking courtiers and trusted family retainers, but she was not encouraged to make friends with them. Every adult in her life contributed to this aura of untouchability, until it was so deeply internalized that it was no longer questioned.

Such is not the case amongst most "ordinary" English aristocrats, even those raised with the great degree of privilege that the Spencer children enjoyed. Royal children, at least in Diana's generation and generations previous, were never permitted to forget that their family stood for something that was greater than the sum of its parts. Their individuality was subsumed in the role they were destined to play, and any attempt to assert individuality was quickly squashed by the machinery of the palace and its army of courtiers who existed for no other purpose than to keep the royals "in line", through oblique criticism and unyielding obsequiousness. A family like the Spencers, on the other hand, were free to enjoy the privileges that came from being born to an ancient and wealthy family line, without the same invisible barrier that divided them from other children their own age. They were not "set apart", save by ordinary social anxieties. As a result, Diana and her siblings grew up privileged, but not snobbish. And while it might be stretching a point to say that the Spencer children were raised with "democratic ideals", the fact that Diana, once she became a royal princess, was famous for having what is called "the common touch", can probably be directly traced to spending her childhood with one foot set in two worlds.

Andrew Morton remarks that "at a very early age the Spencer children had impressed upon them the value of good manners, honesty and accepting people for what they were, not for their position in life." Charles Spencer went so far as to say that he and his sister "never understood the whole title business. I didn't even know I had any kind of title until I went to prep school when I started to get these letters saying; 'The Honourable Charles'. Then I started to wonder what it was all about. We had no idea that we were privileged. As children we accepted our circumstances as normal." From this perspective, one begins to understand how Diana Spencer—daughter of a very old family, familiar with the way things were done amongst the aristocratic classes—found herself capable of socializing on easy terms with members of the royal family once she became older, and why they in turn found something familiar in her, qualities they approved of in a prospective wife of the future King of England.

Diana was not so different, at least outwardly, from Lady Elizabeth Bowes-Lyon, the Scottish aristocrat's daughter who had married the Duke of York and unexpectedly become Queen of England in 1936. But the crucial differences between Diana and her future in-laws, the differences that would make her marriage a misery and her life as a member of the royal family a life-threatening psychological burden, were hidden on a deeper level. The fundamental divide between Diana and the royal family was undoubtedly that early teaching which her husband Charles had received and Diana had not—that royals were set apart from all other species of humans, that their affairs were to be kept private at all costs, domestic disharmony was to be ignored until it simply disappeared or resolved itself on its own, and under no circumstances were outsiders ever to be admitted to the privilege of royal confidence.

The Spencer family's relationship with the royal family began on the most natural of terms—geographically, at least, they were close neighbors. Park House was next door to the 20,000 acre royal Sandringham estate. The royals were in residence there for only brief periods throughout the year, but the Spencers were the sort of family they might safely socialize with, when time permitted. The appearance of a member of the royal family at Park House was a rare event, however, and inevitably found the household unprepared. Princess Anne might send word that she would come to pay them a visit after church, which would send Diana's father scrambling for something to serve her to drink, as he did not partake in alcohol himself. Occasionally the Queen's younger sons, Prince Andrew and Prince Edward, and Princess Margaret's son Viscount Linley, came around to play with the Spencer children, though their visits were not long, nor were they frequent. But the royal family took their social obligations seriously, and the Spencers were invited to Sandringham as often as any of the Queen's neighbors—visits which seemed to inspire a sort of dread in Diana. It wasn't the company she objected to so much as the "strange atmosphere"—not unlike the forbidding, museum-like quality that made their grandfather's seat, Althorp House, a place to be dreaded.

Though the Spencer children played with the Queen's younger sons and nephew, they did not spend much time with Prince Charles. Born in 1948, he was thirteen years older than Diana, and naturally did not spend a great deal of time with the younger children. It was not until her older sister Sarah began dating Prince Charles in 1977 that Diana would meet her future husband for the first time.

Divorce and family break up

In September of 1967, the world seemed to fall apart for Diana and her brother Charles. Their two sisters—Sarah, who was six years Diana's senior, and Jane, four years older than Diana—went away to boarding school. At the same time, the Viscount and Viscountess Althorp decided to end their marriage. Even in the late 1960's, divorce amongst the aristocracy was still a shocking event, especially since Diana's parents had been married in Westminster Abbey in "the society wedding of the year", an event attended by both the Queen and the Queen Mother. Diana's father was twelve years older than her mother, Frances Roche, who was eighteen when they met, one of a sparing crop of post-war debutantes to be presented to society during the austerity of the 1950s. After her marriage to Johnnie Spencer, the most eligible bachelor in his set due to his money, lands, titles, and good looks, the two retired to the countryside to build the 650 acre farm that would eventually surround Park Home. But the pressure for Frances to produce a male heir began almost immediately, and the cumulative toll that it exacted on her, especially after the death of baby John, proved fatal to the marriage. Curiously, Viscount Althorp could not recall any period of particular unhappiness during the 14 years they were together. "How many of those 14 years were happy?" he once remarked. "I thought all of them, until the moment we parted. I was wrong. We hadn't fallen apart, we'd drifted apart."

Diana remembered the latter end of those 14 years of marriage very differently. She recalled that there were violent arguments and shouting in the house from when she was very young. Nevertheless, she was devastated when her parents separated. Frances's reputation suffered a great deal from the stigma of the divorce; she earned the reputation of "a bolter", an old-fashioned pejorative for a woman who leaves her husband and children behind to take up with a more exciting new lover and a life unencumbered by the responsibilities of family. But in fact, she had no intention of abandoning her children, and by the time she had formally separated from John Althorp she had already taken a place in London, with the intention that Diana and Charles should join her there. She had made arrangements for Diana and Charles to start attending nearby schools, and hired a nanny as well. It was a plan intended to preserve as much stability in the children's lives as possible, with weekend visits to their father at Park Home and occasional visits from their father to the house Frances had taken in Belgravia. But ultimately, this arrangement could not be made to work. When the trial separation ended and the couple decided to divorce, Frances sued for custody of her children. She assumed that she would have no difficulty, as mothers were almost always awarded custody of children in such cases. But circumstances conspired against her. The man with whom she had formed a new relationship had been divorced by his own wife, and she had named Frances Spencer as "the other woman" in the case, which reflected poorly on Frances' morals, according to the standards of the times. And then there was the fact that John Spencer was a nobleman by birth, of higher rank than his wife—in the 1960s, the rights of the nobility still outranked the rights of mothers when it came to the custody of children. And finally, Diana's own grandmother sided against her daughter during the custody proceedings and said that the children should be sent to live with their father, a betrayal for which Frances Spencer never forgave her.

It suited the adults in Diana's life to pretend that the children were hardly affected by the divorce at all. The older girls were away at school, so it was easy to pretend that they barely noticed the difference in their family arrangements, while

Charles was only four, and thus deemed too young to care very much. Diana was seven, however, living at home and quite old enough to be sensible of the turmoil—but even where she was concerned, her parents chose to belief that she regarded the break up of the old family routine as "a fresh excitement", rather than a profoundly upsetting trauma. This, of course, flies in the face of our contemporary understanding of early childhood development and the profound and lingering effects that even an amicable divorce can have on children as young as Charles and Diana were, and on sensitive adolescents like Jane and Sarah as well. When Diana was older, she would begin to trace the connection between the upheaval of her parents' divorce and the severe psychological strain she began to suffer from as an adult.

Even in the immediate aftermath of the divorce, the strain on Charles and Diana was palpable to anyone with eyes to see. Both Charles and Diana became intensely afraid of the dark, requiring nightlights to comfort them while the wind howled through the trees of the vast parkland surrounded Park Home. Diana clung to her stuffed animals, and very often she heard her younger brother lying in his bed, crying into his pillow, saying "I want my mummy, I want my mummy." When she could pluck up the courage to brave the darkness of the corridors between their rooms, Diana would go to his bed and lie with him until he fell asleep. Other times she was unable to bring herself to leave her room, and the agony of listening to him cry without being able to help was even worse. "I just couldn't bear it," she would say later. "I could never pluck up enough courage to get out of bed. I remember it to this day." The absence of their mother during the week was rendered all the more painful by the endless procession of nannies, often young, pretty women chosen by their father for their attractiveness rather than their experience or skill in childcare. Some of the nannies were all that a caregiver for lonely children ought to be, and retained close relationships with their former charges long after they sought employment elsewhere, but others were nothing short of abusive. One nanny took to "punishing" the children by putting laxatives into their food, until she was caught in the act by Diana's mother. Others beat the children over the head with wooden spoons, or banged the children's head together. Not all of their nannies were beasts, of course, but it was difficult for the children to trust even the good ones, because, whatever their father might have pretended, it was obvious to them that they had been sent to take their mother's place. Their father was by no means oblivious or unfeeling towards his children, but the divorce had dealt him a severe emotional blow, and he found it difficult to forget his own troubles long enough to relate to them. Charles Spencer recalled that his father "was really miserable after the divorce, basically shell-shocked. He used to sit in his study the whole time. I remember occasionally, very occasionally, he used to play cricket with me on the lawn. That was a great treat."

The aftermath of the divorce naturally made school all the more difficult for Diana, who, though not unintelligent, had difficulty focusing on her lessons, and was prone to outbursts of tears in the classroom. The school she attended provided a fairly gentle, family-like environment, but Diana was set apart by virtue of being the only child there whose parents were divorced. In the 1960s, a divorce was like some dreadful combination of a horrible family tragedy and a lascivious family scandal bound up in one awful, unspeakable affair which could not be alluded to. As Charles grew older, and proved a model student, Diana began to grow jealous because she felt that she could not compete, and the two siblings often got into fights at home. Diana would tackle and pinch her younger brother, while Charles would lash out verbally, calling her slow.

Visits to their mother on the weekends tended to upset Diana and her brother more than soothe them. Either out of a sense of rivalry and competitiveness, or the simple and natural desire to try to cheer the children up, Johnnie Althorp and Frances Shand Kydd (as she was known after her remarriage) positively outdid one another in heaping toys, clothes, and presents on their children. Diana recalled being deeply torn on one occasion, when she was to attend a wedding and had to choose between wearing either the beautiful green dress her mother had given her or the beautiful white dress given to her by her father. She could not recall which dress she had worn in the end, only the sensation that, whatever decision she made, she was committing a terrible betrayal. When Diana and her siblings went to stay with their mother on the weekends, an identical scene played out every Saturday: Frances would greet them at the door to her apartment, and immediately burst into tears. "What's the matter, Mummy?" Charles and Diana would ask, and she would inevitably reply, "I don't want you to go tomorrow". Of course, the children had no choice as to how long they were allowed to stay with their mother, but her emotional outbursts made them feel terribly guilty, as though they were abandoning her.

A certain degree of stability did emerge during their stays with their mother after she was at last able to marry Peter Shand Kydd; he had been a presence in her life for a long time, but until they were officially married, it would have been considered shocking for Frances to have him around the children. Diana and Charles met Peter the very day of his wedding to Frances, and his generous, easy-going nature made him an instant favorite with the children. Charles would later attribute Peter's influence in their life as the source of his sister's easygoing manner towards people from all walks of life: "If you want an insight into why Diana was not just some sort of spoilt toff," he said, "it is because we had very contrasting lifestyles. It wasn't all stately homes and butlers. My mother's home was an ordinary set-up and every holiday we spent half the holiday with our mother so we were in an environment of relative normality for much of our time." The "normality" to which Earl Spencer alludes was still, of course, the normality of the highly affluent; three years after their marriage, Frances and Peter bought a 1000 acre farm in Argyllshire, where Diana had her own pony to ride, and there were ski trips in Switzerland as well. After a particularly bad accident in which Diana fell from her pony and broke her arm, her preferred leisure activities became dance and swimming and tennis. These stood her in good stead when she began attending boarding school at the age of nine.

Diana Spencer's school days

Riddlesworth Hall offered a number of activities that were bound to capture Diana's interest, including prizes for taking care of small animals—she was even allowed to bring her guinea pig, Peanuts, with her from home. Several friends of her own age were also students at the school, and her sister Jane was a sixth form captain, so her father was certain Diana wouldn't be lonely. But at first, Diana saw only that she was being sent away, that the small family unit she had been trying to rebuild in the wake of her parents' divorce was being broken up again. To her father, sending her to school was a natural choice, made in her best interests; to Diana, it seemed that she must have failed him in some intolerable way, and now she was being punished. Unbeknownst to Diana, her father was having almost as much difficulty bringing himself to part with her as she was having in parting with him. "That was a dreadful day," the late Earl Spencer later remarked. "Dreadful, losing her."

Diana had something of a legacy to contend with at Riddlesworth. While Jane was a highly intelligent student who received top marks in her examinations and was renowned for being disciplined and responsible, her oldest sister, Sarah, six years Diana's senior, was the one Diana idolized. And despite the fact that Sarah was in many ways a prize pupil—scoring even higher in her exams than Jane, winning prizes for athletics, a leader of her own set—she had run afoul of the headmistress's good graces by proclaiming herself bored and unchallenged by what Riddlesworth had to offer. The headmistress had suggested that she take a term off, to see what else the world had to offer her. There was much speculation when nine-year old Diana became a Riddlesworth pupil as to which of her sisters she would choose to emulate. The fact was, at home, Diana seemed shy and put-down, the least likely of any of her siblings to make trouble, save when she tussled with

Charles. But in a school environment, especially a boarding school, which is something of its own culture and universe, she found herself emulating Sarah in all of the more mischievous ways and none of the studious, high-achieving ones.

Rather than earning top marks in every subject, as her elder sisters did, Diana remained quiet in the classroom, never volunteering answers or distinguishing herself academically or in extra-curricular activities (save those which involved the care of small animals.) But after school hours, in her dormitory, she was known as someone who like to have a laugh and go in on whatever prank was being cooked up at the moment. She nearly got herself expelled shortly after she started at Riddlesworth by accepting a dare to sneak out of her bed after hours and go in search of extra sweets for the girls to divide amongst themselves. It turned out to be a set up—the girl from the town who was supposed to meet her at the end of the school drive with a box of sweets never turned up—but Diana's absence was noted after one of her fellow students came down with an acute case of appendicitis, sending the whole dorm into uproar. The police had to be called, and when Diana came strolling casually back into her rooms, her headmistress was waiting for her. Diana's parents were called to the school for a stern lecture, which had rather less of a chastening effect on the budding prankster than the headmistress seemed to wish for. Diana's mother and father were not so much concerned that she had slipped out of her room in the middle of the night as they were astonished that their shy, docile daughter turned out to be spirited enough to get up to such high-jinx. As Diana put it:

"I nearly got expelled because one night somebody said to me: 'Would I like to do a dare?' I thought 'Why not? Life's so boring.' So they sent me out at 9 o'clock to the end of the drive which was half a mile long in pitch dark. I had to go and get sweets at the gate from somebody called Polly Phillimore. I got there and there was nobody there."

"I hid behind the gate as these police cars were coming in. I thought nothing more about it. I saw all the lights coming on in the school. I thought nothing about it. I wandered back, terrified, to find that some twit in my bedroom said that she had appendicitis. Then they asked, 'Where's Diana?' 'Don't know.'"

"Both parents, then divorced, were summoned. Father was thrilled and my mother said: 'I didn't think you had it in you.' No telling off."

Diana's poor academic performance at school is something of a mystery. Both her sisters and her younger brother were astonishingly high-performing students, taking the highest marks and winning all the prizes. While Diana admittedly had difficulty in mathematics and science subjects, she was a fluent reader and writer and grasped the intricacies of history and literature. Her school essays in particular showed promise. But the fluency which came so easily to her in school assignments deserted her completely when it came time to sit down and take her formal exams. When it came to O-levels—now called GCSEs, the exams which British students take at age sixteen, after which they may leave school if they choose—Diana was examined in "English literature and language, history, geography, and art". She received D's in all these subjects, which were considered failing grades. It seems likely that Diana's failure to achieve high or even passing grades in these subjects were due more to psychological reasons—a paralyzing fear of failure, perhaps—than to a complete want of ability or intelligence.

Fortunately, Diana found other areas in which it was possible for her to excel. Her athletic accomplishments—she won prizes for swimming and diving—seemed rather poor showing in comparison to her sister Sarah, who had been an outright champion in every athletic endeavor she set her hand to. But Diana had an even rarer and more special gift. Riddlesworth emphasized "good citizenship" alongside academics and athleticism, and there, Diana was a star. Whether she was visiting an elderly lady in her home to do household chores and share cups of tea and biscuits over conversation, or visiting a mental hospital to treat the patients there to a dance, or getting down on her hands and knees to speak face to face with severely disturbed teenagers, Diana's ability to meet the sick and disabled with respect, compassion, and a complete lack of the awkwardness and fear that kept other students at a distance, marked her as a person of very special abilities indeed. Diana's other shining talent was one which she could not pursue professionally, much to her distress—she adored ballet, but because she was over five foot ten, she could never be a professional ballerina.

But she practiced every chance she got, and it became a sort of meditative exercise, taking her away from the trouble in her head. Though she would never be able to perform as part of a professional company, she did win her school's dancing competition in 1976, when she was fifteen.

Chapter Two: Lady Diana Spencer

The death of the seventh Earl Spencer

Diana, her father, and her siblings left Park Home in 1975 and moved to the family seat, Althorp House. Her grandfather had contracted pneumonia and died suddenly, which came as a great shock to his family, because he was strong and vigorous even at 83 years of age. The death of the seventh Earl meant substantial changes in the lives of Diana's family members. Not only did they have to take up residence in forbidding, museum-like Althorp House, they were now all of them titled members of the aristocracy. The children put aside their *Honourables* and became Lady Jane, Lady Sarah, and Lady Diana Spencer. Charles, as the only boy, assumed his father's former title of Viscount Althorp, while their father became the eighth Earl. In order to make the stately old house a little more welcoming for his children, the new Earl had a swimming pool constructed on the grounds. And though Diana was badly homesick for the cozy domesticity of Park House, the domestic staff and servants her father had inherited along with Althorp considered her a sweet darling, considerate and unselfish, and she was soon a great favorite amongst them.

As a young teenager, Diana was just at the age to fall head over heels for the glamorous London lifestyle being led by her eldest sister, whose eighteenth birthday was celebrated at a glorious coming-of-age party hosted by their father. Just as she had been at school, Sarah was one of the leaders of her social set. She dated the most eligible bachelors of the English aristocracy and made her younger sister, who eagerly followed wherever Sarah went, look positively dowdy in comparison. One of Sarah's friends—Lucinda Craig Harvey, who shared a house with Sarah in London and eventually hired Diana as a cleaner at the rather insulting sum of £1 per hour—

remembered the impression that Diana gave as a young teenager: "a rather large girl who wore terrifying Laura Ashley maternity dresses… She was very shy, blushed easily and was very much the younger sister. Terribly unsophisticated, she certainly wasn't anything to look at."

Entranced though she was by Sarah's lifestyle, Diana was still living at home when not at school. The Spencer family unit, which was just beginning to knit itself back together after the divorce and Diana's being sent to school, suffered another serious blow—at least in the eyes of the children—when Earl Spencer remarried. Diana's new stepmother was:

"Raine Spencer, later the Countess de Chambrun…not so much a person but a phenomenon. With her bouffant hairdo, elaborate plumage, gushing charm and bright smile she was a caricature of a countess. The daughter of the outspoken romantic novelist Barbara Cartland [whose novels Diana read enthusiastically], she already had a half-page entry in *Who's Who* before she met Johnnie Spencer. As Lady Lewisham and later, after 1962, as the Countess of Dartmouth, she was a controversial figure in London politics where she served as a councilor on the London County Council. Her colourful opinions soon gave her a wider platform and she became a familiar face in the gossip columns... During the 1960s she became notorious as a parody of the 'pearls and twinset' Tory councilor with views as rigid as her hairdos. 'I always know when I visit Conservative houses because they wash their milk bottles before they put them out,' was one howler which contributed to her being booed off the stage when she addressed students at the London School of Economics."

The immediate antipathy of Diana and all her siblings to Raine Spencer had little to do with her politics, however. When Diana and Charles were introduced to her as pre-teens they promptly declared to their father that if he did marry her, "they would wash their hands of them". Their loathing of Raine was partly due to her high-handed manners, and partly to do with her elaborate plan for reducing the massive death tax penalties their father had inherited by partially gutting Althorp House, selling off many of its antiquities, and opening it part-time as a tourist attraction. However, the worst strike against her came when the children discovered a letter which Raine had written to their father before their grandfather's death. Raine had always made a great show of friendliness towards the seventh Earl and had even helped to effect a partial reconciliation between father and son during the height of their feuding. But the letter which Diana and Charles read revealed that Raine's less than respectful private opinion of their grandfather made her outward show of attention towards him nothing less than hypocritical. Charles retaliated by writing Raine a "vile" letter over his own signature, while Diana tried to persuade one of her school friends to write a threatening anonymous letter to her prospective stepmother. When Raine and Johnnie Spencer did marry, in July of 1977, neither Diana nor any of her siblings were told. Charles only found out when his headmaster at Eton informed him of the news. For the rest of Diana's childhood, she and her brother and two sisters made their stepmother the butt of their jokes and did their best to ignore her whenever feasible.

The "Swan"

Lady Diana Spencer turned 16 in 1977. Though she left school with few academic distinctions, she was made a prefect in her last year—a position of responsibility awarded to senior students in some British schools—and awarded the Miss Clark Lawrence Award for services to the school. All of this, especially being made prefect, made an enormous difference in Diana's self-confidence.

The final stage in Diana's education was a stint at the Institut Alpin Videmanette in Switzerland, a "finishing school" where her beloved sister Sarah had studied briefly. The subjects offered to students at the Institute included "domestic science, dressmaking and cookery", and students were supposed to treat their time there as a full immersion experience in the French language. Diana, however, spent most of her time speaking English with another British student, and devoted most of her energy to skiing. School had nothing more to offer her, and she wrote a number of letters to parents, pleading that they bring her home, arguing that by keeping her there they were only wasting their money. At last, they consented to her leaving, and with her school days behind her at last, Diana began to feel "as if some great weight had been lifted from her shoulders". As Andrew Morton puts it: "She visibly blossomed, becoming jollier livelier, and prettier. Diana was now more mature and relaxed and her sisters' friends looked at her with new eyes. Still shy and overweight, she was nevertheless developing into a popular character. 'She was great fun, charming and kind,' said a friend." Her brother Charles remarked of Diana during this same period that, "Suddenly the insignificantly ugly duckling was obviously going to be a swan."

Early days with Prince Charles

Though Diana had socialized with the Queen's younger children during her early years at Park Home, she did not meet the eldest of them, Charles, Prince of Wales, until 1977, while he was dating her sister Sarah. Charles was—and is—heir to the throne of England, and at the age of 29, was sorely in need of a wife, at least as far as his family was concerned. His options for marriage were wide open. After World War I, King George V, Charles's great-grandfather, had declared that the sons and daughters of English monarchs would, henceforth, be allowed to marry English aristocrats. Previously, only foreign royalty were considered suitable spouses for the sons and daughters of a King, but the war had made it impossible for any English prince or princess to marry a German. The supply of non-German Protestant royalty in Europe had never been very large, and after the war it was even smaller. Charles was therefore free to marry virtually anyone, so long as she was Protestant, had never been divorced, and met with the approval of his family. He was easily the most eligible bachelor in the world, and he was never short of female company. Sarah Spencer was but one in a long string of girlfriends, and her attraction to him was born more of ambition than affection. She was intensely competitive and determined to be the best at anything she turned her hand to—and to be the best at dating, she had to snare the Prince of Wales. It was a simple equation.

Diana was still 16 and a student at school at West Heath when Sarah invited Charles to Althorp House for a visit. It was not, precisely, a fairy-tale meeting of a prince and his destined princess. Charles was addressed, by Sarah Spencer and everyone else in his social circle, as "sir"—the distinction of rank was never forgotten. And the setting was hardly conducive to romance. The Althorp party were in for a rather gloomy afternoon of shooting, and Diana was dressed accordingly, in an anorak, corduroys, and Wellington boots. Sarah had made it clear that Charles was her sphere, off limits to anyone else, including her kid sister. Diana, accordingly, minded her own business and only spoke to Charles when he spoke to her. Charles would later remember the teenage Diana as "a very jolly and amusing and attractive 16-year old—full of fun". He was himself 29 at the time. Diana herself remembered that "the first impact" which her future husband made on her was, "God, what a sad man":

"He came with his Labrador. My sister was all over him like a bad rash and I thought 'God, he must really hate that.' I kept out of the way. I remember being a fat, podgy, no make-up, unsmart lady but I made a lot of noise and he liked that and he came up to me after dinner and we had a big dance and he said: 'Will you show me the gallery?'. I was just about to show him the gallery when my sister Sarah comes up and tells me to push off, and I said 'At least, let me tell you where the switches are to the gallery because you won't know where they are', and I disappeared. And he was charm himself and when I stood next to him the next day, a 16-year old, for someone like that to show you any attention—I was just so sort of amazed. 'Why would anyone like him be interested in me?' And it *was* interest. That was it for about two years."

Sarah Spencer's relationship with Prince Charles was of an on-again, off-again nature, and it would not be long before it was "off" permanently, though the two remained friends. It was a troubled time Sarah's life; she was suffering acutely from anorexia, and had grown so thin that everyone who knew her, especially her family, were deeply worried for her health. (Eventually she was persuaded to enter a hospital for treatment; by sheer coincidence, the psychiatrist who oversaw her care, Dr. Maurice Lipsedge, would, some ten years later, treat Diana for the bulimia which she developed after her marriage.) Sarah was still on sufficiently friendly terms with Prince Charles to warrant an invitation to his 30th birthday party at Buckingham Palace in 1978. Diana also received an invitation, which rather surprised her sister. "Why is Diana coming as well?" Sarah asked, annoyed, to which Diana could only say, "Well, I don't know but I'd like to come." Diana did go, and said later that she "had a very nice time at the dance—fascinating" and that she wasn't the least bit intimidated by Buckingham Palace, only excited and admiring.

It was the party itself, not the prospect of seeing Charles, which had made Diana want to attend. Prince Charles was dating an actress at the time, and Diana wasn't especially interested in dating or romance in general. She was having too much fun enjoying her freedom now that she had finally left her school days behind her. What Diana really wanted at this period in her life was to embark on a career of some sort—preferably working with children—but there were obstacles to this ambition. She had left school without taking any sort of qualifications or receiving any sort of professional training. In this, she was not unique amongst other young women of her social class—old fashioned a notion as it seems today, aristocratic families still cared more for the educations of their sons than their daughters, as it was assumed that, for a daughter, the next natural step after school was to begin socializing with the right sort of people and eventually attract the right sort of husband. Diana wanted desperately to do as Sarah was doing, which was take a house in London and make friends and go to parties. But her parents agreed with the assessment of her last headmistress that she was "rather young for a sixteen-year-old". While they were in no hurry for her to find a husband, they did not relish the notion of their underage daughter bashing about London on her own with no adult supervision. Their verdict was that she would have to wait until she was 18 before she could have an establishment of her own away from the family.

Diana was rather too restless to live with either of her parents full time, particularly her father, since Raine still presided over Althorp House with an iron fist. So for a time, she was sent on long visits to the homes of family friends, until finally her mother gave Diana the use of her own flat in Cadogan Square—a space that Diana could virtually claim as her own, since Frances Shand Kydd spent the majority of her time in Scotland. But though Diana was set for rent and food and most of her clothes, she still needed to earn spending money if she was going to make decisions about purchases without going through her parents. Despite her lack of qualifications, she was able to sign up with a nanny agency, and her older sisters' married friends kept her gainfully employed much of the time as a babysitter. Diana's own needs were modest—she wasn't inclined to attend fashionable parties, except when Sarah insisted that she come along to one of hers to "make up the numbers". Diana preferred to spend her free time reading, watching TV, and having quiet lunches with friends. She didn't smoke, and like her father, never drank alcohol. For a daughter of the wealthy, leisured aristocracy, Diana had an innate wholesomeness that shielded her from picking up a good many bad habits.

A family tragedy imposed itself upon Diana's peaceful existence in the fall of 1978. Her father, Earl Althorp, collapsed suddenly one day from the effects of a massive cerebral hemorrhage. He lapsed into a coma, which was to last for several months. As Diana described to a journalist many years later, her father:

> "...suffered headaches, took Disprins, told nobody. I had a premonition that he was going to be ill whilst I was staying with some friends in Norfolk. They said: 'How's your father?' and I said: 'I've got this strange feeling that he's going to drop down and if he dies, he'll die immediately, otherwise he'll survive.' I heard myself say this—thought nothing more about it. Next day the telephone rang and I said to the lady, 'That will be about Daddy.' It was. He'd collapsed. I was frightfully calm, went back up to London, went to the hospital, saw Daddy was

gravely ill. They said, 'He's going to die.' The brain had ruptured…"

Exacerbating the effects of this shock was Raine Spencer's antagonistic attitude toward her husband's children throughout Earl Spencer's illness. She was herself completely devoted to the Earl's care and recovery, but she seemed to feel that visits from his daughters and son would only endanger him further. Diana went on to describe how she "saw another side" of her stepmother which she "hadn't anticipated":

"…she basically blocked us out of the hospital, she wouldn't let us see Daddy. My eldest sister took charge of that and went in sometimes to see him. Meanwhile, he couldn't talk because he had a tracheotomy so he wasn't able to ask where his other children were. Goodness knows what he was thinking, because no-one was telling him. Anyway, he got better and he basically changed character. He was one person before, and he was certainly a different person after. He's remained estranged but adoring ever since."

It was, however, probably due to Raine's devotion that the Earl *did* recover. After learning of a new drug developed in Germany which was not yet licensed for use in Britain but had been helpful in cases similar to her husband's, Raine reached out through her many highly placed contacts and arranged for the Earl to receive the experimental treatment. It was successful in rousing him from his coma, and though he had a long convalescence to face, he went on to live another fourteen years.

During her father's illness, Diana found herself understandably out of sorts, even less able to focus on building some sort of career for herself than she had been before. She was, at the time, enrolled in a cooking school, an institute where girls from the "velvet hairband" set—daughters of the aristocracy who were mostly biding their time until they were suitably married—paid large sums in order to learn the finer points of sauces and soufflés. Diana was not making much success of it. Thanks to her mother, however, Diana enjoyed a brief stint working at the job of her dreams, as a grade two ballet teacher for children. Her employer was Betty Vacani, famous for having been a dance instructor for three generations of royal children. Diana's time at the school lasted for only three months, however; during a skiing trip, she suffered a fall which resulted in her tearing all the major tendons of one of her ankles. She had months of convalescence to face, and she would never again have the dexterity to teach ballet.

Coleherne Court

When Diana turned 18, her parents gifted her with a house of her own in London, at Coleherne Court. Diana was ecstatic; ever since she had left finishing school in Switzerland, she had wanted nothing more than an independent establishment of her own in London. Long ago, she had promised one of her best school friends that as soon as she had her own house, there would be a place for her in it, and Diana was as good as her word. She claimed the house's largest suite for herself, but she took on her three closest friends as roommates, charging them a paltry £18 a month in rent. As landlord, Diana exerted herself only so far as to make up a chore rota to ensure that everyone pitched in with keeping the house tidy. But there was little enough mess, especially in the kitchen—though two of the girls, including Diana, had attended *cordon bleu* cooking courses, none of them ever cooked meals to eat at home. Diana could make one or two dishes rather well, however, including borscht soup and a chocolate ganache, and these dishes were in popular demand with her friends, who would ask her to pop around to their flat and deliver them for dinner parties.

Diana's social life during her single year of post-school independence was that of a young, privileged, innocent teenager. She lived with her closest friends and socialized a good deal with young men of their social set—brothers of girls she'd gone to school with, sons of the aristocracy who had gone to Eton and were working in their father's firms by day, and looking for a bit of jolly company in the evenings. These young men were much more like playmates to Diana, at least, than they were like boyfriends. Though one or two of these young men were seriously interested in Diana, she considered herself far too young and naïve to deal with the complications of a serious romance, or even casual sex. She was still a virgin when she married Prince Charles—a deliberate choice on her part, because she had always felt that she would probably marry someone very much in the public eye, and it would be better if she didn't have any awkward encumbrances in her past that might embarrass her future husband. "She was very sexually attractive," one of her former friends remarked, "and the relationship was not a platonic one as far as I was concerned but it remained that way. She was always a little aloof, you always felt that there was a lot you would never know about her." By 1980, another of Diana's boyfriends, Adam Russell, returned to England after spending a year travelling, and he had all but determined to ask Diana to marry him when he next saw her. But when Russell asked a mutual friend whether Diana was seeing anyone at the moment, the friend told him: "You've only got one rival. The Prince of Wales."

Prince Charles comes courting

"All the world and the glory of it, whatever is most attractive, whatever is most seductive, has always been offered to the Prince of Wales, and always will be. It is not rational to expect the best virtue where temptation is applied in the most trying form at the frailest time of human life." Walter Bagehot, an eminent Victorian constitutionalist, wrote these words in the 19th century, but they remained true as of 1969, when Prince Charles was invested as Prince of Wales. He was a "charming male chauvinist", as one of his friends put it, and he expected the women in his life—and there was never a lack of them—to come when he called, suit themselves to his schedule, watch appreciatively as he played polo, dine with him when he wanted company, and generally be at his beck and call. He had his own schedule of daily activities, and the women who lasted longest in his life were those who simply rearranged their schedules around his. Those who could not or would suit their lives to his lost his interest, and he tended to drop them very coldly and quickly. But this was partly because he had already met the love of his life, a woman it seemed he would never be able to marry, and his search for a wife was therefore a pragmatic affair, rather than a quest for romance.

Prince Charles had met Camilla Shand, now the Duchess of Cornwall, in 1970, at a polo match. A romance developed quickly between them, only to falter after Prince Charles joined the royal navy. Camilla, thinking their relationship was over, married Andrew Parker-Bowles in 1973. At some point between her marriage and Charles' first encounter with Diana in 1977, Camilla and Charles rekindled their romance, though the Prince's official biographer asserts that they did not begin to have an affair until 1986, five years after Charles and Diana had wed. It may well be that Charles and Camilla's relationship was not sexually intimate when Charles was courting Diana, but Camilla was deeply involved in Charles's life, and their devotion to one another was an open secret amongst their own circle of friends. She had habit of vetting his girlfriends, approving this one or that one as potentially suitable suitable wives.

It was no doubt a thankless task for Charles, providing himself with a wife who would be the future Queen of England and the mother of the future King, when he only wanted to carry on as he had been doing with Camilla. He and Camilla seemed to have missed their opportunity—now that she had married another man, Charles would not be able to marry her unless she was widowed, and Charles's family was hardly prepared to wait for that eventuality. The Duke of Edinburgh has referred to his son as "a romantic", but for a long time Charles was seen as anything but, due to the public statements he made regarding the business of marriage. Forced to adopt a pragmatic view of things, he said that "Marriage is a much more important business than falling in love." He added, "I think one must concentrate on marriage being essentially a question of mutual love and respect for each other... Essentially you must be good friends, and love, I'm sure, will grow out of that friendship. I have a particular responsibility to ensure that I make the right decision. The last thing I could possibly entertain is getting divorced." He had good reason to feel that divorce was impossible; the last member of the British royal family to divorce was Henry VIII.

Even if he could not be with the woman he truly loved, Charles clearly at least hoped to find a marriage partner with whom he could share a certain degree of warmth, affection, and camaraderie. He had one or two serious relationships with women prior to Diana that might have fit the bill, including one with the granddaughter of Lord Mountbatten, who had been the adoptive guardian of Prince Philip, and had been chiefly responsible for arranging Philip's marriage with the Queen. But Lord Mountbatten was assassinated before his marriage scheme for Charles could come to pass, and ironically, it was his death that led to Charles' choosing Diana.

Despite his devotion to Camilla Parker-Bowles, Charles was strongly attracted to Diana from the moment of their first meeting when she was 16, and much more so when they met again some two and a half years later. Diana herself had sensed that he was rather fascinated by her at the time, though she struggled to account for such a reaction, considering the difference in their ages. But it is quite possible that Diana reminded Charles a bit of Camilla, or at least that she brought some of the same qualities out in him that Camilla did. Prince Charles has been said to share some commonalities of temperament with his great-uncle, the Duke of Windsor, whose abdication in 1936 to marry Wallis Simpson was still hanging like some dreadful shadow over the Queen as she fretted over Charles's marital prospects.

Both Charles and his great-uncle were inclined to depressions and melancholy, and depended on the company of devoted female friends to make them optimistic and cheerful. Camilla excelled at lifting his spirits, and since her marriage to Charles in 2005 it has been observed that she always brings a much-needed note of tasteful humor to royal occasions, and that the Prince seems "lighter" in her company. The teenage Diana no doubt provided Charles with a similar sort of light-heartedness. Unlike almost all the other women Charles came into contact with at that point in his life, she didn't want anything from him. As the kid sister of his girlfriend, she certainly had no ambition to marry him. She was not impressed by his being royal, only by the fact that he was a proper grown up, while she was still a child. Her sense of fun, her aptitude for pranks, and her general lack of self-consciousness must have made her company something of a relief for Charles, who was perfectly aware that most women he met saw him as a prize to be snared. He was so much run after by women in general that he probably could not fathom that any young woman he knew could look at him without hoping that he would pay special attention to her. But Diana hadn't the slightest notion of how profound an impression she had made on the Prince at Althorp in 1977 until a few years later. Diana's obliviousness regarding his interest in her made Diana quite mysterious to Charles—and therein, it seemed, lay the attraction.

In 1979, Diana was both startled and excited when the Queen invited her to spend Christmas at Sandringham with the royal family. It would mean seeing a good deal of Charles, but that wasn't the appeal, for Diana. Rather, as an eighteen-year old, she felt that she was being taken seriously as an adult for the first time, that after years of being included in invitations sent to her parents she was being singled out for her own sake. She still hadn't the slightest idea that Charles was at all interested in her. There is a now famous story told about the moment Diana shared the news of the Christmas invitation with one of her friends. At the time, she was on her knees, wearing yellow rubber gloves, cleaning the kitchen floor. She looked up and said, "Guess what? I'm going on a shooting weekend to Sandringham!" Her friend, who was a touch more sophisticated than Diana, replied, "Gosh, perhaps you are going to be the next Queen of England." Diana's only response was to laugh. "I doubt it. Can you see me swanning around in kid gloves and a ball gown?"

Diana seems to have developed a certain fondness, or at least sympathy, for Prince Charles during the Christmas visit. The assassination of Lord Mountbatten, who was his godfather, had deeply upset him, and Diana naturally had compassion for people who suffered great loss. Not long after the Sandringham Christmas visit, Diana found herself receiving another invitation that would throw her into Charles's company—and this invitation would set the course for the rest of her life.

"I was asked to stay [with friends] in July 1980," Diana recounted. "'Would you like to come and stay for a couple of nights down at Petworth? Because we've got the Prince of Wales staying. You're a young blood, you might amuse him.' So I said 'OK'. So I sat next to him and Charles came in."

Charles's interest had apparently become obvious to Diana while she was at Sandringham, and when they met again she found that it had only intensified. "He was all over me again and it was very strange," she said. "I thought, 'Well, this isn't very cool.' I thought men were supposed not to be so obvious, I thought this was very odd. The first night we sat down on a bale at the barbecue at this house... I said: "You looked so sad when you walked up the aisle at Lord Mountbatten's funeral.' I said: 'It was the most tragic thing I've ever seen. My heart bled for you when I watched. I thought, 'It's wrong, you're lonely—you should be with somebody to look after you.'"

To Charles, who depended on the attention of women to keep his spirits up, and who had always found his own mother to be rather cool in her affections towards him, it was as if a fuse had been lit. "The next minute," said Diana, "he leapt on me, practically, and I thought this was very strange, too, and I wasn't quite sure how to cope with all this. Anyway we talked about lots of things and…that was it. Frigid wasn't the word. Big F when it comes to that."

It was scarcely surprising that she was flummoxed by the ardency of his attentions, but she was equally taken aback by Charles' expectation that she, like all the other women in his life, would mold her schedules and activities to his expectations. "He said: 'You must come to London with me tomorrow. I've got to work at Buckingham Palace, you must come to work with me.'" Diana refused, thinking that it would rude to her hosts if she slipped away with no explanation. "I said: 'No, I can't.' I thought 'How will I explain my presence at Buckingham Palace when I'm supposed to be staying with [their mutual friend, Philip de Passes]?'" But Charles's mind appeared to already be made up that Diana was the right candidate for the job vacancy of future Queen of England, and from that moment forward, his presence dominated her life. He began inviting her to accompany him on multiple outings, usually in the company of his friends, who were all Charles's age or much older. The eighteen-year old Diana, who still rather in awe of the Prince of Wales, was also dismayed by the way his friends treated her, as though they knew something she didn't. And, of course, they did. They were aware that Charles had singled Diana out in a far more serious way than he had ever done with any of his other female companions and that the only explanation must be that he intended to marry her. Diana, however, had trouble believing that his intentions could be so serious. She felt in over her head, but at the same time, too star struck by the Prince to resist being dragged along.

In September of 1980, Prince Charles invited Diana to Balmoral, the enormous, sprawling estate in the Scottish Highlands acquired by Queen Victoria, which has served ever since as the royal family's most cherished family retreat. It is traditional for members of the royal family to invite friends and romantic interests to Balmoral as a sort of test to see how they get on with the larger royal circle. It is said that anyone who passes "the Balmoral test" is in with the family for good, while anyone who fails it disappears quietly. As it happened, Diana's brother-in-law, Jane Spencer's husband, was a member of the royal household, and as such, the couple had their own cottage on the grounds, which meant that Diana could stay with them and avoid the nerve-wracking challenges of navigating a stay in the main house. As it happened, Diana passed the family test, but she was about to embark on a whole new ordeal. Journalists with long-lens cameras spotted her when she accompanied Charles on a fishing trip. They were unable to identify her, as Diana slipped away quietly with a scarf over her head, but the sighting had proven that there was a young woman in the Prince of Wales' life. Shortly after Diana returned to London, the journalists figured out her identity—and from that moment forward, her anonymity was gone forever.

Diana's persecution at the hands of the tabloid press during the brief period she and Prince Charles were dating is by now legendary, as it is impossible not to draw a connection with the manner of her death in 1997—killed in a traffic accident while trying to evade the paparazzi. But in 1980, Diana could not even attempt to evade the reporters. They gathered in huge swarms outside her Coleherne Court house and the kindergarten where she worked as a teacher. They followed her and her housemates wherever they went and rang her phone at all hours of the day and night. They were desperate for information about her relationship with the Prince—how did they meet, was it serious, did she want to be Queen, were they engaged yet. Buckingham Palace courtiers considered it inappropriate to make any sort of statement about the relationship until Charles and Diana were officially engaged, and Diana was still too over-awed by Charles—she still called him 'sir'— to explain to him the full scope of the problem.

The press, however, was a mere inconvenience in the grander scheme of things. Diana was frequently harassed by them to the point of nervous tears, but she and her housemates also enjoyed cooking up schemes to outwit them. To make dates with Charles, Diana once resorted to climbing out her window down a rope of knotted bedsheets and crawling over dustbins, while on other occasions her roommates acted as decoys and drove Diana's car in one direction while Diana left the house on foot and walked in the opposite direction a few minutes later. The more serious issue in her relationship with Charles was the very great inequality that existed between them—not in terms of rank so much as power. The press was hounding the royal family as well, but they possessed the well-oiled machinery of palace staff to buffer them from the onslaught. Diana had no such resources, nor were the royal family willing to use theirs on her behalf. More importantly, Diana was so young, and so completely without experience of romance, dating, or men, that Charles controlled all aspects of their relationship by default. He set all their dates, and he made certain they were never alone together. His friends, who were all older and more sophisticated than Diana, were always present during their outings. This gave Diana little opportunity to get to know Charles as well as she wished. But within a month or so of the beginning of their courtship, Diana found herself hopelessly in love with her royal suitor. She did not blame him for the difficulties he thrust her into, and in fact, she thought that he was the one who deserved to be pitied, because of all the hard work and tedious demands that came with his position. She was now determined to do whatever it took in order to make the relationship work, even if that meant behaving like "his willing puppy that came to heel when he whistled", as one of Diana's biographers puts it. Aware of the disadvantages that came with being so inexperienced, Diana turned to her three housemates for advice. They had all stood by her loyally through the ordeal of her courtship, and they were all more experienced in dating than Diana was. And it was to them that she turned once Diana realized that some of Charles's behavior was peculiar even by the standards of royal princes.

For instance: one of the "new friends" Diana made when she became a part of Charles's social circles was Camilla Parker-Bowles and her husband Andrew. She spent a great deal of time at their house, and Camilla seemed to make a point of seeking her out, giving her advice about the best way to manage Charles. What Diana found strangest of all was the fact that, any time Diana and Charles discussed something in private, Camilla seemed to know the details. Naïve though Diana undoubtedly was, even she understood that something must be going on between Charles and Camilla. She had once asked Charles about his past girlfriends, and he had told her, quite candidly, that most of his relationships had been with married women, because they were "safe"—they would never be able to marry him, so they were unlikely to put pressure on him or do damage to their own reputations by going to the press. Diana was just beginning to put two and two together. Charles had clearly been interested in her since that Christmas at Sandringham, and they had begun to date officially in July. It was now February of the following year, and, in Diana's words, "the feeling was, 'I wish Prince Charles would hurry up and get on with it.' The Queen was fed up."

Diana knew that the Queen was pressuring Charles to settle down, but she did not know that Charles's father, Prince Philip, had written him a letter early in 1981, telling him that, having dated Diana for so long, he owed it to her to either propose, or "let her go", for the sake of her own reputation. The Duke of Edinburgh had rather old-fashioned sensibilities, and he was aware that Diana was not like his son's sophisticated, ambitious former girlfriends, but rather a sheltered, virginal teenager who would probably go on to marry someone else important if Charles wouldn't have her. Friends of Charles who read the Duke's letter thought that it was fair and reasonable, but Charles took it as a bullying ultimatum. He was neither prepared to marry Diana nor to let her go. And even if he did let Diana go, he would only have to marry someone else that wasn't Camilla, and soon—he was already 33, which was three years older than the age at which he had publicly remarked it would be a good idea to settle down. He decided to propose, but it was not an entirely willing or enthusiastic decision.

Diana described in an interview what happened next, from her perspective:

> "Charles rang me up from Klosters [in Switzerland, where he was skiing with friends] and said: 'I've got something to ask you.' Instinct in a female, you know what's coming. Anyway, I sat up all night with my girls, saying 'What do I say, what do I do?'—bearing in mind that there's somebody else around. By that time I'd realized that there *was* somebody else around. I'd been

staying at Bolehyde with the Parker-Bowleses an awful lot, and I couldn't understand why she kept saying to me, 'Don't push him into doing this, don't do that.' She knew so much about what he was doing privately, and about what *we* were doing privately… I couldn't understand it."

Ultimately, however, her suspicions were not as strong as her love for Charles—or her belief that Charles loved her, despite whatever bond he might feel towards his former girlfriend Camilla. Charles invited Diana to Windsor Castle after his return from Klosters. He took her up to the nursery, told her that he had missed her very much while he had been away—and then, without further preamble, asked her to marry him. Diana thought it was a joke at first, despite her earlier "intuition", and laughed, saying, "Yeah, ok." Charles affirmed that he was serious, and this time, Diana said yes with the appropriate gravity. Anxiously, he pointed out that marrying him would mean she would be

Queen one day. Diana later said that she knew, instinctively, in that moment, that she never would be Queen. But she told him that she loved him, and Charles said, quite famously—he would repeat himself during a later television interview—"Whatever love means." He left the room to phone the Queen and tell her that Diana had accepted his proposal, and Diana returned to her home to share the news with her friends and housemates:

"I came back to the flat and sat on my bed. 'Guess what?' They said: 'He asked you. What did you say?' 'Yes, please.' Everybody screamed and howled and we went for a drive around London with our secret. I rang my parents the next morning. Daddy was thrilled. 'How wonderful.' Mummy was thrilled. I told my brother [that she was engaged] and he said, 'Who to?'"

Diana's brother, Charles, expounded on his reaction: "When I [heard the news] she looked absolutely blissful and was beaming away. I just remember her as really ecstatic... From the baptism of fire she had got from the press she knew that she could handle the role too. She looked as happy as I have ever seen her look. It was genuine because nobody with insincere motives could look that happy. It wasn't the look of somebody who had won the jackpot but somebody who looked spiritually fulfilled as well."

The one member of Diana's family who was not enthusiastic was her maternal grandmother, Ruth, Lady Fermoy, who had been lady-in-waiting to the Queen Mother. After years of service with the royal family, she knew them quite well, and she had uttered a rather prophetic warning when Diana first began dating Charles that Diana recounted much later: "My grandma always said to me: 'Darling, you must understand that their sense of humor and their lifestyle are different and I don't think it will suit you." Diana's sister Jane, whose husband was the Queen's assistant private secretary, had a similar level of familiarity with the royal family, and was just as concerned as their grandmother, but there was nothing that she or anyone could do about it. Diana was to be the next Princess of Wales and eventually Queen of England—and that, it seemed, was that.

Chapter Three: Princess of Wales

Engagement

There was a brief period of respite between the day that Diana accepted Charles's proposal—February 6, 1981—and the day that the engagement was officially announced by Buckingham Palace on February 24th, during which Diana took a ten-day trip to Australia with her mother and step-father. There, they discussed wedding plans, and Diana began trying to wrap her head around the enormity of the change that was about to overtake her life. She was naturally quite nervous, and she missed Charles dreadfully, but her new fiancé was mysteriously unavailable to help soothe her during this trying time. Diana explained that:

"I pined for him, but he never rang me up. I thought that was very strange, and whenever I rang him up he was out, and he never rang me back. I thought, 'OK.' I was just being generous— 'He is being very busy, this, that, and the other.' I come back from Australia, someone knocks on my door—someone from his office with a bunch of flowers. And I knew that they hadn't come from Charles, because there was no note. It was just somebody being very tactful in the office."

The night before her engagement was announced, Diana moved to Clarence House, which was the Queen Mother's official residence. This move reflected the official change in her status: as soon as the official announcement was released, she would no longer be a private person, but the Princess of Wales in waiting, a possession of the Commonwealth, like the rest of the royal family. She would be under constant guard by a Scotland Yard police detective, and her leaving Coleherne Court for Clarence House was "expected", partly for her own safety and partly to keep up appearances. Her Scotland

Yard bodyguard pointed out to her, perhaps not helpfully, that "this is the last night of freedom ever in the rest of your life, so make the most of it." Diana said later that she felt as if a sword had gone through her heart.

Once the official announcement was made, Diana found herself swept into a world that seemed to consist only of anxiety and stress. She developed a severe case of bulimia which would plague her for years to come. The weight loss was extreme—she lost six and a half inches of waistline between the day of her engagement and her wedding day. Her only consolation was tearful phone calls with her old friends at Coleherne Court, who watched with deep concern as Diana seemed to waste away before their very eyes. One of her housemates, Carolyn Bartholomew, recalls that after Diana went to live in Buckingham Palace, "This little thing got so thin. I was so worried about her. She wasn't happy, she was suddenly plunged into all this pressure and it was a nightmare for her. She was dizzy with it, bombarded from all sides. It was a whirlwind and she was ashen, she was grey."

The Queen, anxious to help Charles's bride-to-be prepare for her role, assigned Diana her favorite lady in waiting, Lady Susan Hussey, as a guide and companion. But Lady Susan, a dyed in the wool royal supporter, painted a picture of royal existence that Diana found very grim and difficult to accept—one in which all individuality is submerged into the institution that is the monarchy. Diana resisted Lady Susan's lessons, which was to prove a harbinger of the lifelong resistance she would field against the expectations imposed upon her as a royal personage. A popular thread of feeling in Diana's mythos is that the royal family in general were as unsupportive as Charles undoubtedly was during their engagement and afterwards, but the truth is rather more complicated. With regards to the Queen specifically, the dominant concern of her entire life since she came to the throne at the age of 25 has been to preserve the British monarchy—which was practically the only powerful monarchial house in Europe still standing by the time the second World War came to an end. It would have been disastrously stupid for the Queen to ignore Diana or fail to do what she could to prepare her for public life as a member of the royal family, and in fact, she did not ignore her. But the Queen's concern was to help Diana learn how to fit in with the rest of the family, to perform to their expectations, and Diana found Lady Susan's lessons dismaying.

Though she would not articulate the sentiment until a decade later, Diana's love of Charles was not the only reason she married him—she also felt a strong sense of calling to public service, a calling she knew she would be able to serve as Princess of Wales. In many ways, this ought to have made her a natural fit as a royal, but Diana was not willing to surrender her own ideas about what public service should entail to the carefully tailored agenda of charitable concerns vetted by the Palace, as an ideal royal would. Diana did not always find Palace approval for the causes she wished to champion, such as destigmatizing AIDS, but she championed them anyway. Diana's biographer, Andrew Morton, who is her fierce partisan, asserts that "Diana was given less training in her new job than the average supermarket checkout operator", but this assessment fails to account for the fundamental clash in ideologies that led Diana to resist the training that the Queen attempted to provide.

Charles, on the other hand, bore a great deal of responsibility for failing to provide Diana with the emotional support that might have made her more willing to compromise and adjust her expectations of royal life. He was himself so distressed by the fact that he was about to marry a woman other than Camilla that he consoled himself by spending increasing amounts of time in Camilla's company during the engagement. And Camilla was continuing to offer what Diana considered a peculiar and almost invasive level of advice and support now that the engagement was official. As Diana recounts:

"When I arrived at Clarence House there was a letter on my bed from Camilla, dated two days previously, saying, 'Such exciting news about the engagement. Do let's have lunch soon when the Prince of Wales goes to Australia and New Zealand. He's going to be away for three weeks. I'd love to see the ring, lots of love, Camilla.' And that was—'Wow!'"

Uncertain what else to do, Diana took Camilla up on her invitation:

"I organized lunch… I was so immature, I didn't know about jealousy or depressions, or anything like that. I had such a wonderful existence, being a kindergarten teacher—you didn't suffer from anything like that, you got tired, but that was it. There was no one around to give you grief. So we had lunch. Very tricky indeed. She said: 'You are not going to hunt are you?' I said: 'On what?' She said: 'Horse. You are not going to hunt when you go and live at Highgrove, are you?' I said: 'No.' She said: 'I just wanted to know,' and I thought, as far as she was concerned, that was her communication route."

Diana's suspicions about Charles's relationship with Camilla, which had started prior to the engagement, were all but verified as the wedding date approached. Charles was scheduled to take a five-week tour of Australia in March of 1981, and just before he left, he received a phone call from Camilla in his office, while Diana was present. She wasn't certain how to behave—she sensed that Charles would react badly if she questioned his desire for a private chat with another woman, so she decided to simply take herself off to another room and let them say their farewells. But the reaction to the scene caught up to her after she watched Charles's plane take off. She was famously photographed breaking down into tears after he kissed her goodbye, but she was weeping because she now knew for a certainty that she was as good as trapped in an engagement with a man who was in love with another woman.

Shortly before the wedding took place, Diana opened a package which had been delivered to Charles's office and discovered a woman's bracelet which had been engraved with the intertwined initials "F" and "G"—which Diana knew stood for "Fred" and "Gladys", Charles and Camilla's nicknames for one another. It was tantamount to evidence of their affair, and abruptly, the patience and meekness and awe of Charles which had stopped her from ever questioning him before gave way to anger. She demanded an explanation; she demanded that Charles not give Camilla the bracelet. "Why can't you be honest with me?" she pleaded. But Charles insisted that he was going to give Camilla the bracelet, and he refused to answer any questions or have any kind of discussion about his relationship with her. Diana's conclusion was that "he had made his decision, and if it wasn't going to work, it wasn't going to work"—in other words, he had selected Diana for the honor of being his wife and future Queen, but if she wanted it, she would have to tolerate his relationship with Camilla. "He'd found the virgin," Diana said, "the sacrificial lamb, and in a way he *was* obsessed with me. But it was hot and cold, hot and cold. You never knew what mood it was going to be, up and down, up and down."

When Charles left the office in a huff to go and have lunch with Camilla, where he would present her with the bracelet, Diana went upstairs to have lunch with her sisters. She explained to them what had happened—and she came extremely close to calling the wedding off: "I can't marry him," she told them, "I can't do this, this is absolutely unbelievable." Her sisters were sympathetic, but they understood all too well that Diana was trapped—canceling the wedding at this point would have been a scandal of epic proportions. "Well, bad luck, Duch," they told her. (Diana's childhood nickname was "Duchess".) "Your face is on the tea-towels, so you're too late to chicken out." Diana laughed through her tears, but the tears returned in buckets later. The night before the wedding, Diana received her own gift of jewelry from Charles—a signet ring engraved with the Prince of Wales' emblem, along with a card, which read: "I'm so proud of you and when you come up I'll be there at the altar for you tomorrow. Just look 'em in the eye and knock 'em dead." It was a sweet and tender note, and it calmed Diana's apprehensions temporarily. Then, at dinner that night, she suffered her first binging and purging episode—the start of the bulimia that would plague her for the next decade.

Princess of Wales

Diana described her wedding as "the most emotionally confusing day" of her life: "I was very calm [the morning of the wedding] when we were getting up at Clarence House... I was very, very calm, deathly calm. I felt I was a lamb to the slaughter. I knew it and couldn't do anything about it. [I'd had] my last night of freedom with Jane at Clarence House..."

The night before the wedding she hadn't had any sleep because she had been placed in a bedroom in Clarence House where the windows overlooked the streets, and the masses of cheering crowds kept her awake all night. Her exhaustion no doubt contributed to the deathly calm she felt as she was guided through preparations for the ceremony. The walk down the aisle at St. Paul's was the most taxing walk she ever took in her life: her father, Earl Spencer, was to give her away, but he had great difficulty walking due to physical impairments resulting from the aneurysm he had suffered years earlier. Diana would have to be his crutch, bearing most of his weight on her arm, and there was deep concern that he might not make it the whole length of the aisle. As Diana and her father made their excruciatingly slow progress, Diana found herself looking out across the sea of wedding guests, looking for Camilla: "I knew she was in there, of course."

A sense of unreality pervaded the entire occasion. "I thought the whole thing was hysterical," said Diana. "Getting married... it was so grown up, and here was Diana—a kindergarten teacher..." But despite the insecurity which made her search the crowd for

Camilla, she was "so in love with my husband that I couldn't take my eyes off him. I just absolutely thought I was the luckiest girl in the world." She had tremendous hopes for her future with Charles, despite everything. She felt that "he was going to look out" for her, like any fairy tale prince would do for his princess. Yet her optimism was mingled with an equally profound sense of ambivalence and uncertainty. Leaving St. Paul's was "a wonderful feeling, everybody hurraying, everybody happy because they thought we were happy"—but was Diana truly happy? "There was the big question mark in my mind. I realized I had taken on an enormous role but had no idea what I was going into—but *no* idea."

During Charles and Diana's honeymoon tour, Diana's bulimia, which had been mild up to that point, worsened severely, as she began bingeing and purging four to five times a day. She startled domestic staff by turning up in the kitchens at all hours for casual chats and between-meal snacks. She was so skinny that everyone was baffled by the size of her appetite, but no one guessed the truth—in 1981, the details of how eating disorders like bulimia and anorexia function were not widely understood, and even medical professionals tended to misunderstand them. In fact, it is partially because of Diana that there is a much greater degree of public awareness regarding bulimia now than there was 36 years ago. But it was almost inevitable that her eating disorder, which was founded on a profound sense of loss of control, would be triggered during the course of the honeymoon, since her new husband displayed continual proofs that Camilla Parker-Bowles was still at the forefront of his mind. On one occasion, when Diana and Charles were comparing their schedules, two photographs of Camilla fell out of Charles's diary; on another, Diana spotted Charles wearing cufflinks engraved with two "C"s interlocking, like the Coco Chanel logo. Charles admitted that they had been a gift from Camilla, but he still refused to discuss the nature of their relationship or his feelings for her. As far as Charles was concerned, his relationship with Camilla was like the locked room in the tale of Bluebeard's wife—Diana only attempted opening it at her peril.

After the honeymoon

Diana believed, as did the rest of the royal family, that the intense media obsession with her, which had been relentless during Charles's courtship, would fade after the public had been given the meaty public spectacle of a fairy tale wedding between prince and princess. Everyone thought that life would return to normal, or as normal as royal existence ever was. It was therefore quite baffling—to Diana more than anyone—that her celebrity status only grew more pronounced. She was the only royal anyone cared about anymore. Despite her aristocratic background, she was seen as common because she did things like open doors for herself; this made her seem relatable, or attainable, so the appetite for details about her life and personality only grew more insatiable. Anyone who had ever known her was approached by journalists for stories.

Yet it wasn't truly Diana anyone was interested in, but the Princess of Wales, a position into which she had been placed like a mannequin displaying a dress. A year before her marriage she and her housemates had been sneaking off to their boyfriend's houses in the middle of the night to throw eggs at their cars as a prank—but this was not the person the public wanted to know. Unfortunately, at the exact point in her life when she most needed people to see her for who she was, she was surrounded exclusively by people who saw only a Princess, who was to be handled with kid gloves, rather than given honest and sensible advice. She was too well-bred to let her emotional turmoil show in public, but in private she was falling apart, and was no longer able to hide this fact from the royal family. Her love for Charles was constantly at war with her jealousy and suspicions about Camilla, and the result was that "she lived on an emotional see-saw". There were brief periods of happiness, when she and Charles were alone together and she accompanied him on long walks around the Balmoral estate, or lay out on blankets while Charles read passages from books aloud to her. But these were only short respites between long periods of agony.

Diana's bulimia continued to intensify, and as her physical health deteriorated, her ability to regulate her emotions deteriorated as well. Her royal in-laws were not, as they have often been depicted, cruelly callous towards her suffering, but they were poorly equipped to understand or help her. The Queen, and all her children, had been raised to contain their feelings, no matter how distressing they were, and rely on the structure of their highly regimented existence for stability. Even with their closest friends and loved ones, they did not pour out their troubles to listening ears. It was assumed that Diana would learn how to adapt to this mode of existence. But not only had she been raised with the values of a different era (the royal family was quite literally Victorian in many of its habits and sensibilities, and even the younger members were extremely old fashioned), she did not have any kind of stability to cling to while she attempted to sort through her feelings. The other royals had each other, their identity, their traditions. Diana should have had Charles, as her guide into this framework, but she didn't, at least not full time. There was no one in whom she could confide. Charles's family naturally took Charles's side, and her own family, as much as they loved her, were too aristocratic in their own sensibilities to do anything but tell her that she must get on with it as best she could. Her best friends, the residents of Coleherne Court, could have given her the sort of advice she needed, but

Diana couldn't bear to burden them. They, like the rest of the world, believed in the story that was being told about Diana's marriage in the newspapers, that of the greatest fairy tale in modern times. She couldn't bear to disappoint them by admitting that it was all a façade.

Charles, though he refused to address the fundamental root of Diana's insecurities by speaking with her honestly about his relationship with Camilla, tried to help in other ways. He was well aware of the bulimia by this point, as well as her intense anxiety. A great believer in therapy and psychiatric medicine, he arranged for her to see various professionals—doctors, counselors, authors of books on psychology. But Diana seemed unable to benefit from therapy, probably because she saw the doctors as being on her husband's side, and she adamantly resisted their efforts to prescribe medication for her. The professionals who were treating her wanted to place her on sedatives, because they believed that she needed relief from her intense anxiety before any progress could be made. They probably were not wrong about this, but it is also true that in the 1980s sedatives were highly overprescribed by today's medical standards, especially to women, and especially to wealthy women whose husbands had a position to maintain. If Diana felt that Charles and the doctors he consulted were trying to control her response to his infidelity by drugging her into submission, she might not have been entirely wrong. In her own view, she "did not need drugs, she needed rest, patience and understanding from those around her." But the highly public life she was now leading left little space for rest, and the royal family's patience began to wear thin when she failed, as they saw it, to cooperate with her doctors or make any progress in overcoming her problems—and they were *her* problems, in their eyes, although the Queen was extremely angry about Charles's relationship with Camilla. The Parker-Bowleses had once been frequent visitors to the Palace and attendees at royal functions, but the Queen issued a blanket order that "that woman"—the phrase which the royal family had once employed to refer to Wallis Simpson—was not to set foot in any royal residence or be admitted to any royal event. She could not forbid Charles from seeing her, because she knew he would not listen, but her name was not to be mentioned in the Palace.

Diana might eventually have capitulated to pressure and allowed herself to be medicated, and medication might or might not have helped her to begin recovering from her bulimia and anxiety. But then, in October of 1981, Diana discovered that she was pregnant, and this gave her an iron-clad excuse to avoid all psychiatric medications—she could not risk any harmful side-effects to her baby, not when she was carrying the future King of England.

Chapter Four: A Decade of Marriage

Crisis days

"I threw myself down the stairs [at Sandringham]. Charles said I was crying wolf, and I said I felt so desperate, and I was crying my eyes out, and he said: 'I'm not going to listen. You're always doing this to me. I'm going riding now.' So I threw myself down the stairs. The Queen comes out, absolutely horrified, shaking—she was so frightened. I knew I wasn't going to lose the baby; quite bruised around the stomach. Charles went out riding and when he came back, you know, it was just dismissal, total dismissal. He just carried on out of the door."

Thus Diana described the first of many suicidal gestures and incidents of self-mutilation which arose out of the bitter desperation she was feeling in the first months of her marriage to

Charles. It was January of 1982, and she and her husband had spent most of the family holiday at Sandringham having screaming, hysterical fights in their suite, fights which could be heard from all the way down the corridors. She was three months pregnant with William but she was thinner than she had been before the pregnancy, due to morning sickness and the frequency of her purging episodes. Charles's patience and attempts to be helpful and understanding had given way to disgust, exasperation, and ultimately dismissal. He did not believe there was anything wrong with his wife; he thought she was making herself sick on purpose to manipulate him, to make him feel guilty enough to stop seeing Camilla, whom he still refused to discuss with her. When she threatened to kill herself just after New Year's, Charles refused to take the threat seriously, and stalked off to go riding. After Diana threw herself down the staircase, her doctors were promptly summoned to make certain neither she nor the baby were harmed, but Charles only continued to ignore her.

More such incidents followed. She threw herself into a glass display case at Kensington Palace, cut herself with razors and vegetable peelers and during one fight with Charles even stabbed herself with a small knife, while he looked on. "His indifference pushed her to the edge," remarked one person who observed their domestic spats—and it was all the more tragic, because Diana loved Charles so much that if he had taken a different approach with her, she probably would have done anything he wanted. But Charles seemed to take Diana's problems as a personal insult. It was as if, in his mind, he had made her Princess of Wales and asked nothing in return save that she do her duty and ignore his affair with another woman. But Diana was too ill to perform her official duties without paying a huge physical and emotional price. Her pregnancy with their first son, William, was very difficult, no doubt all the more so because of her bulimia, but the royal family were poorly equipped to understand why this should interfere with her duties—none of the women in their family had ever had morning sickness like Diana's. Ironically, Prince William's wife, Katherine, Duchess of Cambridge, suffered so much from morning sickness with her first pregnancy in 2013 that she had to be hospitalized—but the fact that this was permitted was a sign of how differently things are done in the royal family nowadays than they were in 1982. In fact, the Duchess probably benefited from the lessons which the royal family learned during their years of dealing with Diana.

Diana was terrified of disappointing the royal family by failing to fulfill her public duties, so despite the fact that she had always been nervous when she was the center of attention, and despite how desperately ill she felt, she forced herself to carry out the ceremonial visits and speeches and all the rest. She had a remarkable talent for putting on a smile and completely disguising how horrible she felt before the cameras, but there were often tears and meltdowns in the car before Charles could persuade her to get out and face the public. At home, the fact that she often had to leave the dinner table to be sick made her feel, correctly, that Charles's family was coming to regard her as a problem to be dealt with. No matter how difficult her official responsibilities were—such as the time she had to deliver a speech that was partially in Welsh—and no matter how well she performed her public responsibilities, she received no acknowledgment or thanks from her husband or his family. Perfectly performed duties were unremarkable. Only failures were noticed.

Prince William

Diana's difficulties with her pregnancy were exacerbated by the unrelenting scrutiny of the media. Besotted from the start with their fairy tale princess, the obsession took a dark and invasive turn after Diana, five months pregnant, was photographed in a bikini during a holiday with Charles. For once, Diana, Charles, and the Queen were all on the same side: the newspapers had officially gone too far. The Queen instructed her press secretary to summon Fleet Street editors to the Palace, where he made an official request that Diana's privacy be respected, for the sake of her own health and that of the baby she was carrying. Nothing changed, however. Pressure mounted to such a degree that Diana decided to induce labor as her due date approached. She had moderate anxieties about the health of her child, remembering all too well how the death of her infant brother John had cast a permanent shadow over her family, but she had a strong instinct that her own baby was, in her words, "well cooked", and was ready to greet the world.

Unlike the Queen, who had given birth to her own children in her own bedroom in Buckingham Palace, Diana gave birth at the hospital. The delivery was, proportionally speaking, as difficult as the pregnancy had been, despite Diana's receiving an epidural. The labor carried on for so long that doctors were considering an emergency Caesarean section; she was continually sick through the delivery and her temperature spiked to dangerous heights. But finally, her child was delivered safely at 9:00 on June 21, 1982, and when the Queen got her first look at him, she smiled and remarked that it was a blessing the baby didn't have his father's large ears. It took a few days to settle on the new Prince's name—he was called "Baby Wales" in the mean time. Diana was the one who chose the name William; Charles had wanted to call him Arthur, so that became his second name.

There was a brief period of happiness and respite after William's birth. Charles was delighted by the birth of a son and heir and occasionally deigned to change diapers, which was very hands-on for a man who did not run his own baths. Diana made clear to the nanny that her child was not to be kept exclusively in the nursery and trotted out only for brief, scheduled visits. Traditionally, the children and grandchildren of the monarch had been raised almost entirely by nannies and educated by governesses until they went to boarding school— a great deal of distance would arise between parent and child unless the parents took care to make those visits count, as was the case with the Queen's parents. As a child, the Queen had been brought up by the same nanny who had raised her own mother, and Charles wanted William, and later Harry, to be raised by Mabel Anderson, the nanny who had looked after him. He also wanted to have the boys educated at home by governesses until it was time for them to go to boarding school, as he and every royal prince of recent generations had been. But Diana had a vision for how she wanted her sons to be raised. Having been brought up in an old-fashioned aristocratic style herself, passed from one nanny to the next, then to boarding school, she knew that the inevitable result was emotional deprivation at a time in a child's life when affection and consistency are most important. And she was determined that her children should be brought up in a manner that differed, at least slightly, from the traditional royal model. As she put it:

"I *am* altering it for [William], but in a subtle way; people aren't aware of it, but I am. I would never rattle their cage, the monarchy, because when I think the mother-in-law has been doing it for 40 years, who am I to come along and change it just like that? But through William learning what I do, and his father to a certain extent, he has got an insight into what's coming his way. He's not hidden upstairs with a governess."

That William and Harry not be "hidden away" was crucial to Diana. A former kindergarten teacher herself, she wanted her children to attend nursery school with other boys and girls their age. The aura of being set apart which surrounded the royal family was in part a product of being raised so differently than everyone else. Diana was determined that her sons would not be entirely out of touch with normal life. They would always be different from other children, and William needed to keep to some traditions so that he could be prepared for becoming King. But Diana would see to it that William and Harry would be their mother's sons, as well as royal princes.

Turning point

When William was still only a few months old, Diana and Charles made an excruciating six-week tour of Australia and New Zealand. When the Queen was just a baby, her parents, then the Duke and Duchess of York, embarked on their own foreign tour, and left her behind in the care of her grandparents and nannies for several months. The Queen herself, along with the Duke of Edinburgh, left England for a tour of Australia in 1954, leaving Prince Charles and his sister Princess Anne behind with their governess. As if upholding tradition, the Duke and Duchess of Cambridge also made a tour of Australia in 2014, when their son Prince George was less than a year old. But the tradition of leaving the children behind was broken by Diana and Charles, who were particularly invited by the Australian prime minister to bring William along with them. William followed in their footsteps by bringing Prince George along on his own tour.

The grueling pace of the tour was very difficult for Diana to maintain; it also exhausted her ladies-in-waiting. William spent most of the trip with his nanny, and Diana was only able to see him for brief periods of time when she had the rare break, but it was a comfort to her knowing that he was only a car ride, rather than a plane ride, away. In addition to the stress imposed by the arduous physical demands of the six-week tour, a new element of emotional strain interposed itself between Diana and Charles. All his life, Charles had been the star of his own show, the person the crowds flocked to see and wave and cheer for. Even when he appeared in public with other members of his family, he did not suffer greatly in comparison. But now that he was traveling with his wife—"Princess Di", the glamorous but unwilling face that sold a million magazines—all the crowds wanted to see was *her*. When they drove down the streets, the people who had lined up on Charles's side would groan in dismay and remark that they'd picked the wrong side, that it was Diana they'd come to get a glimpse of. The crowds were utterly enormous—more than a million people came out to see the royal couple, and this in a country with a total population of only 17 million. Almost all of them had come to see Diana.

Charles was completely unprepared for finding himself suddenly so demoted, playing second fiddle to a wife who, in his view, was making life a misery for them both. In public, he joked graciously about it, commenting that he knew his place, that he was only there as his wife's escort. In private, he was petulant. It did not help when Diana, who was bewildered and harassed by the amount of attention she was receiving, protested that the last thing she wanted was to be the star of any sort of show. Even when she was a child, she would only participate in school pageants if she could play non-speaking roles. It was only because she was a novelty, she tried to explain; they would have been equally interested in whomever the Prince of Wales had happened to marry. But Charles remained irritable.

Despite the fact that she spent most of the Australia tour feeling sick, harassed, and unfairly treated by her husband, Diana emerged afterwards a changed woman. Since the beginning of her marriage, she had looked to Charles for guidance as to how she ought to behave. Now she knew that she could handle even the most arduous of official royal functions. She had acquired a new skill set, and with it came greater confidence. Isolated from all her former friends since her marriage, she began to reach out to them again. Initially, she had not been able to face them—hearing the mundane details of their own lives would have reminded her of the freedom she had lost, and she could not bear to confess to them that her fairy tale marriage was a miserable sham. But reconnecting with her friends was a way of reconnecting with the sense of self she had lost when she married into the royal family, and it did her good to see and speak with them.

Prince Harry

"Between William and Harry being born it is total darkness," Diana recalled in 1992. "I can't remember much, I've blotted it out, it was such pain." She was, perhaps, better than she had been—she had reconnected with friends, discovered that the police detectives who were assigned to her protection detail were usually excellent allies and sources of advice, and begun taking on solo engagements representing the royal family. But she was also convinced that Charles was seeing Camilla in secret. It was one thing to know that they had feelings for one another, and something else to believe they were spending happy hours in each other's company while she fretted those same hours away next to the telephone every time Charles was late coming home. Yet, somehow, despite her mistrust and apprehensions, "Harry appeared by a miracle." Diana stated that she and Charles "were very very close to each other the six weeks before Harry was born, the closest we've ever, ever been and ever will be."

Yet as happy as Diana and Charles were to be having another child, Diana knew that another crisis was looming on the horizon. Charles badly wanted their second child to be a daughter, Diana "knew Harry was going to be a boy because I saw on the scan… I didn't tell him." Charles made no attempt to hide his disappointment when he saw his new son: "Harry arrived, Harry had red hair, Harry was a boy. First comment was, 'Oh God, it's a boy.' Second comment, 'and he's even got red hair.'" No one in recent generations of the royal family had ever had red hair, but Diana's brother and sister did. It was as if Charles's disappointment was augmented by the evidence that the baby had Spencer blood. He quickly left the hospital to play polo. His cold attitude, his indifference to Harry, proved to be the breaking point. Once sick with love for her husband, Diana was now, effectively, cured. "Something inside me closed off," she said. At Harry's christening, Charles told Diana's mother: "I'm so disappointed—I thought it would be a girl." It was a deeply insensitive thing to say to a woman who had lost her one of her children to fatal birth defects when he was only ten hours old, and Frances Shand Kydd "snapped his head off," according to Diana, and told him, "You should be thankful that you had a child that was normal."

Confrontation and breakdown

In 1986, Sarah Ferguson, a distant cousin and good friend of Diana's, married Charles's brother Prince Andrew, becoming the Duchess of York. "Fergie", as everyone called her, was an instant hit with the royal family. She seemed to be Diana's opposite in every way—blooming with energy and good health while Diana was sickly, weak, and always tired—and everyone was quick to make comparisons at Diana's expense. "Why can't you be more like Fergie?" Charles once asked Diana. In fact, Diana had a similar prankish sense of humor to her sister-in-law, but it had been completely smothered by five years of royal existence. Hoping to win approval, and perhaps a bit relieved by the prospect of letting her hair down after so long, Diana began to incorporate a bit more jollity into her life. She started going out more, playing pranks with her new sister-in-law, socializing with friends outside of the royal circle, attending rock concerts, and generally trying to emulate Fergie's carefree attitude. There was immediate backlash. The newspapers turned on Diana overnight, criticizing her "frivolity", deeming it inappropriate when she giggled nervously during troop inspections. More exasperating than all the rest was the endless speculation that arose any time Diana was spotted attending a concert or dining or dancing at a party with a man other than Charles. Whenever she was photographed in male company, it was made to seem as though these friendships were evidence of marital discord and salacious affairs. It particularly galled Diana when she received a grilling in the newspapers for dancing with various men at the same party where Charles had spent hours ensconced in conversation with Camilla.

Even as Diana's frustration mounted over her seeming inability to do anything right in the eyes of the press or her husband or his family, two events occurred which altered her attitude towards her position and alleviated her sense of powerlessness. The first event involved the tragic death of Charles's equerry, Major Hugh Lindsay, who was killed in a sudden avalanche while he was on a skiing holiday in Switzerland with Charles, Diana, Fergie, and others. Everyone was extremely shaken. Charles in particular was in shock, as was Fergie, who was then six months pregnant. Diana alone managed to remain perfectly calm and make sensible decisions, gathering Lindsay's effects to return to his wife, and organizing the party's immediate return to England. Though Diana was as grieved as the others by Lindsay's death, the fact that she was able to effectively take charge and make useful decisions bolstered her confidence enormously.

The second event was a short conversation with one of her closest friends, Carolyn Bartholomew. Deeply concerned by Diana's poor health, she had done research into bulimia and had been horrified by what she read about the long term medical consequences of the disease when left untreated. She told Diana that if she did not immediately seek treatment, she would go to the press, effectively blackmailing Diana into taking the first step towards recovery. What Bartholomew had realized was that, even though Charles's infidelity was the root cause of her depressions, suicide attempts, and self harm, the severity of her emotional instability was due in large part to the fact that her body was starved of nutrition. Dr. Maurice Lipsedge, the same doctor who had treat her sister Jane for anorexia, told Diana that if she could avoid purging most of the time for six months, she would feel like a completely different person. In the mean time, he gave her books to read about eating disorders. People with mental health conditions who receive a diagnosis and begin to research their illness for the first often experience what one psychologist calls the, "Ah! It's me!" effect. Diana had to read the books that Lipsedge gave her in secret, lest anyone see the titles and draw conclusions, but she read them with fascination, excited and relieved to realize that she was not the only person who had ever suffered with such an illness, that it was an understood and researched condition experienced by many people.

Diana continued to experience purging episodes when she was trapped in anxiety-inducing circumstances, but when things were fairly normal, she began to find that she could keep her food down. And the doctor's prediction proved accurate—mental stability began to return as her body grew stronger. With this newfound strength, Diana made a fateful decision: she determined to have a frank conversation with Camilla Parker-Bowles. She knew that it would be awkward, that Charles would furious, and Camilla possibly resentful. But Charles had never been willing to acknowledge his affair or discuss his feelings on the subject, so Diana felt entitled to discuss the matter with the other person involved. She had been invited to attend the birthday party of Camilla's sister, but it was assumed that she would not attend. When she did turn up, there was visible surprise and tension amongst the party guests. Diana was composed and gracious, waiting for her opportunity. Eventually, she registered the fact that Charles and Camilla had slipped away downstairs, so she decided to go and join them. Diana recounted walking in on:

"...a very happy little threesome going on downstairs—Camilla, Charles and another man chatting away. So I thought, 'Right this is your moment,' and joined in the conversation, as if we were all best friends. The other man said, 'I think we ought to go upstairs now.' So we stood up and I said, 'Camilla, I'd love to have a word with you, if it's possible,' and she looked really uncomfortable and put her head down. I said to the men, 'Boys, I'm just going to have a quick word with Camilla... I'll be up in a minute.' They shot upstairs like chickens with no heads, and I could feel upstairs all hell breaking loose, [as if the guests were saying] 'What's she going to do?'"

Diana had carefully considered what she wished to say to Camilla, and she had made up her mind not to cause a scene, or lay any blame for her marital unhappiness at Camilla's door. The point of the conversation, as she saw it, was simply to take control of the situation in the only way she knew how. It was now 1988; she had been married to Charles for seven years, and his affair with Camilla had been an obsession since before Charles even proposed. In confronting Camilla, she was laying the matter to rest in the only way she knew how:

"I said to Camilla, 'Would you like to sit down?' So we sat down. I was terrified. I said, 'Camilla, I would just like you to know that I know exactly what is going on between you and Charles, I wasn't born yesterday.' Someone was sent down to relieve us, obviously [someone had said], 'Go down there, they're having a fight.' It wasn't a fight—calm, deathly calm. I said to Camilla, 'I'm sorry I'm in the way. I obviously am in the way, and it must be hell for both of you, but I do know what is going on. Don't treat me like an idiot.'

"In the car on the way back, my husband was all over me like a bad rash, and I cried like I have never cried before—it was anger, and it was seven years' pent-up anger coming out. I cried and cried and cried and I didn't sleep that night. [But] the next morning, when I woke up, I felt a tremendous shift. I'd done something, said what I felt. The old jealousy and anger [were still] swilling around, but it wasn't so deathly as before. I said to him at the weekend three days later, 'Darling, I'm sure you'll want to know what I said to Camilla. There's no secret. You may ask her. I just said I loved you—there's nothing wrong in that… I've got nothing to hide. I'm your wife, and the mother of your children.'"

Over the next few years, the "tremendous shift" which Diana experienced after confronting Camilla led to an intensive regime of spiritual exploration and physical fitness, which were to help her face the intense ordeal that was to come as her marriage to Charles entered its final disintegration, leading to separation and ultimately divorce.

A new purpose

In the early 1990s, as Diana began to feel centered in herself for what was quite possibly the first time in her life, she discovered something like a calling—a way in which she could use her position to be of service to people, to fulfill her lifelong sense that she had "a role to play". It began after Charles broke his arm in a polo accident in 1990. The break was severe and required multiple surgeries and a stay in the hospital. While Diana was there to visit him, she found herself superfluous, and decided to stop in and visit some of the other patients. One of these was a woman who had collapsed suddenly three days earlier with a brain hemorrhage and now lay dying in a hospital ward, with her husband in the chair beside her, holding her hand. Diana asked if it would be all right if she joined him. She took the chair on the other side of the bed and held the woman's other hand, until the doctor came into the room and pronounced her dead a few hours later. Diana consoled the family, and sent them a note after the funeral. Afterwards, she realized that she was in a position to bring great comfort to people who were suffering, and to use her position to bring greater attention to the causes of suffering. She began consulting with religious leaders such as the Archbishop of Canterbury as to how she could assist the sick and the dying: "Anywhere I see suffering, that is where I want to be, doing what I can," she told him. She began visiting hospitals, and in 1991, accompanied by First Lady Barbara Bush, she visited an AIDS ward. In 1991, before drugs such as AZT and Prep became widely available, AIDS was still a death sentence, and because it was stigmatized as the "gay disease" during a time when homosexuality was still largely taboo, there was not nearly enough public interest in funding the necessary research into treatment.

AIDS research and the plight of AIDS patients would become one of Diana's most passionate causes. Before Diana could represent the royal family in public, for any reason, she had to ask the Queen's permission. When she approached the Queen regarding her desire to become involved in AIDS awareness, the Queen asked her, wearily, "Can't you do something nice?" Her attitude was no more than typical of the times, and she has since acknowledged privately that she was mistaken, and that Diana's decision to champion the cause of AIDS research probably had a great deal to do with the advancements that were made in treating the disease over the next twenty years.

In Edinburgh, in 1993, Diana gave a speech regarding the plight of women and children with AIDS. At the time, it was not widely understood that HIV, the virus which causes AIDS, was more than a sexually transmitted disease affecting gay men, but a blood-borne virus which could be spread to anyone who came into contact with affected fluids. Diana's speech, reproduced below, helped to foster the understanding that AIDS had to be treated as a public health crisis, rather than a plague visited on society's "deviants":

> Some sections of the media would have us believe that the dark shadow of AIDS is fading away. The predicted explosion has failed to happen and retreated back to those who've so often been condemned or ignored.
>
> Yet common sense and the testimonies of healthcare workers, worldwide, tell us a very different story. The truth is, that most people infected by HIV are heterosexual and the disease is spreading, throughout the world, at a staggering rate.
>
> By the year two thousand - only seven years from now - even the most conservative estimates predict there will be more than thirty million people, worldwide, with

HIV - equivalent to more than half the population of the United Kingdom.

Mothers and children are being infected; or are affected by the Aids virus in greater and greater numbers, every single day.

A mother with HIV or Aids doesn't give up the responsibility of caring for her children easily. Often she is the sole parent, the wage earner, the provider of food, the organiser of daily life, the nurse to other sick members of the family, including her own children. Relentless demands continue to be placed on her, at a time when her own health and strength are falling away.

As well as the physical drain on her energy, a mother with HIV carries the grief and guilt that she probably won't see her healthy children through to independence. If she has passed on HIV to one of her children, she will have to witness their illness while trying to make something of their short life. Worrying as to what will happen to them if she dies first.

Trying to plan for her surviving children's futures won't be an easy task. At what stage should she give up her role as a parent? Who can she rely on to take care of them? Where can she find the right kind of support to decide what is best for them? How can she be sure that her family history and traditions won't be lost?

Yet the biggest fear of the mothers I've met with HIV or AIDS is not their disease. They've learnt to live with their disease, especially, as for much of the time they are feeling well. No, what terrifies them most, is other people. For despite information about Aids being available now for nearly ten years, these women still face harassment, job loss, isolation, even physical aggression, if their family secret gets out.

How then is it possible for them to decide the moment to explain to their children what is happening in their lives? Do they tell the neighbours? Do they tell their children's school? Is there anyone they can truly trust or is it safer and wiser to struggle on alone?

Yet these mothers don't ask for sympathy. Their need is for understanding. To be allowed to live a full and active life. To be given the support to love and care for their children, for as long as they can, without carrying the added burden of our ignorance and fear.

And what of the children who live with HIV every day? Not because they're necessarily ill themselves, but because their family life includes a mother, father, brother or sister who has the virus. How will we help them come to terms with the loss of the people they love? How will we help them to grieve? How will we help them to feel secure about their future?

These children need to feel the same things as other children. To play, to laugh and cry, to make friends, to enjoy the ordinary experiences of childhood. To feel loved and nurtured and included by the world they live in, without the stigma that AIDS continues to attract.

By listening to their needs, really listening, perhaps we can find the best way of helping these children to face their future with greater confidence and hope.

The effect HIV and AIDS has on mothers and children, when the disease is allowed to spread unchecked, was brought home to me on my recent visit to Zimbabwe. I saw for myself the very personal tragedies whole families were suffering.

The damage it was doing to their communities, to the country as a whole, both socially and economically, was devastating.

Yet the support these families were given by those around them was a lesson for us all. They were being treated with compassion and respect, by their friends and neighbours, for what they were having to go through. And were still accepted as an important part of their community, not as outcasts to be ignored.

Here in the United Kingdom the number of women and children known to be infected or affected by HIV or AIDS is still comparatively small. But if we continue to believe that AIDS is someone else's problem, we too, could so easily be facing the same devastating destruction of our nation's way of life that is already happening in other parts of the world.

In my daily life I've seen for myself the tremendous work being done by the many charities and government organisations who are searching for new ways of tackling the dilemma of AIDS. The importance of this conference, here in Edinburgh, cannot be underestimated. It brings together those people who represent milestones of achievement around the world in dealing with the complexities of HIV and AIDS in mothers and children. And also, those who've pushed back the boundaries of our understanding of how the infection is transmitted and how it can be treated. Your exchange of ideas and experiences will, I am sure, make a difference to the future well-being of us all.

I feel certain, we as a nation still need to develop a deeper understanding of what AIDS really is. To possibly, be just a little more aware and just a little less embarrassed about how the virus is transmitted, even when we don't really see ourselves at risk. In that way, perhaps, we may play a small part in helping to protect a person we love from becoming infected with HIV.

For those mothers and children already living under the dark shadow of AIDS we need to help them back into the light. To reassure them. To respect and support their needs. And maybe, we will learn from them, how to live our own life more fully, for however long it is.

Charles was not impressed by Diana's work caring for AIDS patients—which included personally, secretly, nursing a close friend through the final stages of the illness for the last several months of his life, even bringing William to see him so that the young prince could begin to understand what the illness meant and how it affected people. As Diana continued to involve herself personally in the plight of the ill and the dying, the media took notice and praised her for her efforts. Charles, as was always the case when the media made much of his wife, accused her of acting like a martyr. Their marriage, which was approaching its tenth anniversary, was by now over in all but name. Charles and Diana could no longer maintain even the pretense of a cordial professional relationship.

The public had long been given reasons to suspect that there was tension in the marriage of the Prince and Princess of Wales, but those suspicions were all but confirmed in 1992, when Diana's father, Earl Althorp, died while she on a skiing trip with Charles, William, and Harry. Diana began making preparations to leave, expecting that Charles would stay where he was with the boys, and she was annoyed when Charles insisted that he should accompany her. She informed him that it was "a bit late to start acting the caring husband". Charles, along with his press secretary, argued with her for hours that it would do great damage to Charles's image if he was not seen at his wife's side at the funeral, but Diana wanted to mourn her father in private without the stress of having to pretend that her husband's presence was in any way a comfort to her. She only agreed that he should return to England after the Queen's intervention was sought; she ruled that Charles must go, so Diana capitulated. But no sooner did they arrive in the country than they went their separate ways.

When Charles came to the funeral, he arrived separately from Diana.

Only a few years earlier, Diana would wait nervously by the phone when Charles was late returning home. Now, being in the same building with him made her unbearably anxious. They were leading separate lives to the greatest extent possible. Separation crossed her mind almost daily, but it seemed an impossibility, for many reasons. One of the most important was that, unlike almost any other woman in the country, Diana could not reasonably expect to be awarded custody of her children by default. Just as the divorce courts had granted the aristocratic Earl Spencer custody of his four children, the royal family had undisputed possession of the two princes. Another reason was Diana's deep sense of duty towards the Queen. Diana had promised her that no matter what happened she "would not let her down"—that is, walk out.

This resolve was tested when the marriage of the Duke and Duchess of York disintegrated in 1992, after only five years. Fergie, who was, like Diana, an outsider who had married into the royal family, was better placed than anyone else to understand the miseries of Diana's marriage, and her longing for freedom. She begged Diana to join her in making her escape, but Diana was determined to cling on if she could. It was the position, not the husband, which mattered to her now. Besides, Diana had seen the way in which the Duchess was treated by Palace courtiers after her separation. As one BBC news report said, "The knives are out for the Duchess at Buckingham Palace." Diana knew that the knives would be even sharper in her case, if she dared make her own bid for freedom.

Chapter Five: The People's Princess

Diana: Her True Story

The Duke and Duchess of York had announced their formal decision to separate on March 19, 1992. It was the first in a series of disasters for the royal family which would lead to the Queen, in her Christmas speech at the end of the year, to refer to 1992 as her "annus horribilis", Latin for "year of horrors". She had good reason to feel that way. A month after the Yorks' separation, Anne, the Princess Royal, received a divorce from her husband, Captain Mark Philips, making her the first member of the royal family to divorce since Henry VIII. Then, on June 8, Andrew Morton's book *Diana: Her True Story,* was published.

The impact of Morton's biography of Diana can scarcely be overstated. Not since Marion

Crawford published her memoir about the childhoods of Princess Elizabeth and Princess Margaret against the express orders of the Palace had so much information about the royal family's private lives been made available to the public. And while the Queen was undoubtedly the Diana of her day, making *The Little Princesses* an instant best-seller, Marion Crawford's sentimental memoir contained only the lightest criticism of any member of the royal family. Morton's book, by contrast, pulled back the bed hangings and overturned the dustbins on the marriage of the Prince and Princess of Wales. Unauthorized books about the royals were published fairly regularly, based mostly on gossip, media reports, and anecdotes winkled from low-ranking members of the Palace staff. Morton's book took its information straight from the horse's mouth—Diana, desperate to tell her side of the story after years of having it told for her by the newspapers and by the Palace, cooperated fully with the writing of the book and authorized her closest friends and family to speak to the author.

There would be no end to the trouble Diana would find herself in if it were known that she had authorized the writing of the book, so deniability was maintained at all times. She met in secret with a go-between who interviewed her on Morton's behalf and brought the tapes back to him. This was so that Diana could say, with perfect truth, that she had never met nor spoken with Morton, and Morton kept secret the full details of her participation in the book's publication until after Diana's death. The need for secrecy was paramount. The book made the Prince of Wales look callous, deceitful, shallow, spoilt, and even cruel, and it painted the rest of the royals as indifferent, at best, to Diana's intense suffering in the early days of her marriage. In short, the book's publication was regarded as the monarchy's greatest crisis since the abdication of King Edward VIII in 1936. The details it provided were so intimate that the Palace immediately suspected Diana of being involved in its writing, but she denied it, and there was no proof, nor any way of getting the cat back into the bag.

The threat which *Her True Story* represented to the Palace and the Queen rests in the fact that, in this day and age, the monarchy exists only by the consent of the people of Britain—it is the last great monarchial house in the world, but Queen Elizabeth, now in her 90s, is old enough to remember vividly when all of Russia and Europe were still ruled by royal houses, and how they toppled, one after another, during the years just before and after World War II, as waves of populist rebellion swept the continent. Nearly everything that seems peculiar, out of touch, and antiquated about the royal family can be explained by the Queen's deep belief, instilled in her by grandmother, Mary of Teck, who was a protégé of Queen Victoria, that the monarch and her heirs must conduct themselves in a highly specific manner in order to maintain the public favor that is necessary to their existence. Amongst other things, that code of behavior demanded avoidance of scandal at all costs.

When it came to the monarchy's relationship with the public—that is, its popularity—Diana had, quite without meaning to, upset the whole ship of state, from the very beginning of her marriage. Polls continually reflected the fact that "Princess Di" was the royal family's most popular member, by a considerable margin. If the fate of the monarchy depended on public favor, then the fate of the monarchy depended on Diana, who had won the love of the public without even trying. There had been resentment over this fact for a long time, but after *Her True Story* was published, it was as if a saboteur's bomb had exploded in the corridors of Buckingham Palace. Diana had for so long been painted as the vapid princess, concerned only with clothes and frivolous, shallow pursuits, her friendships with men blamed for the discord in her marriage, that it was natural for her to want to tell her side of the story. But it is also natural that the royal family felt betrayed and threatened.

The very day after the book began to be serialized in the *Sunday Times*—June 8, 1992—Diana and Charles met at Kensington Palace for a surprisingly cordial conversation about how to proceed. They concluded, mutually, to do as the Duke and Duchess of York had done, and start a formal separation. The Queen, however, insisted that they first take a period of three months in which to at least attempt to patch things up before she would countenance. Dutifully, Diana and Charles carried on with the usual public façade—but open warfare was soon to break out between them.

The Wars of the Waleses

It wasn't long before the attempt at reconciliation, which included a miserable family trip to the Bahamas which the Palace attempted to bill as a "second honeymoon", collapsed under scandals and smear campaigns. In the first two months after *Diana: Her True Story* was published, the *Sun* published transcripts of illegally recorded phone calls between Diana and a close male friend which made it clear that the two had been having an affair at the time it was recorded a few years prior. At the same time, Charles's coterie of close friends and hangers-on—a group Diana referred to as "the Highgrove set", as their social center was Charles's home, Highgrove—began making their own comments to the media, hinting that Diana was so mentally deranged as to have broken from reality completely, and that the picture painted of Charles in Andrew Morton's book was a product of those delusions. Charles and Diana discussed separation with the Queen once more, and she agreed to an informal separation, in which the two would lead separate lives, reuniting only for the most important royal functions, such as Trooping the Colour.

But even this was not an effective solution—Diana and Charles argued bitterly over who would live in which palace, whose staff would move out of which office, and most importantly, who would have custody of the children. Diana's threats to take William and Harry and move to Australia were met with reminders that the royal family is governed by a set of laws that apply to no one else in Britain. Diana's children belonged to the Commonwealth as much as to her; they must stay in England. Finally, in December of 1992, Prime Minister John Major made the public announcement that the Prince and Princess of Wales had agreed to a formal, official separation. Diana deliberately arranged the timing of the announcement so that the worst blowback would be over before William and

Harry left school for the Christmas break, since their boarding school environment insulated them from the media coverage. Henceforward, during school terms, she and Charles would see them on alternate weekends.

By 1994, Charles had a biography of his own to match Diana's. *Prince of Wales: A Biography,* by Jonathan Dimbleby, was written with Charles's full cooperation and with Buckingham Palace's blessing. Diana had told her side of the story of their marriage to Andrew Morton in order to set the record straight after years of being misrepresented in the press. Dimbleby's book was Charles's attempt to answer the extremely unflattering portrait that Diana and Morton had painted of him. Whether or not one is inclined to side with Charles over Diana, there is no denying that *Prince of Wales*, by its merits, is simply a less compelling book than Morton's vivid and emotionally brutal insider portrayal of royal life. This is due mostly to the fact that the author took exceptional pains to avoid anything that hinted of criticism of his subject, which the notoriously thin-skinned Charles could not tolerate.

The book was unable to win public opinion back over to Charles's side. The British public were outraged over the revelation that Charles had been unfaithful, but Charles seemed to believe his actions would be met with understanding if he simply explained to Dimbleby that he had felt pressured, even bullied into marrying Diana, despite the fact that he badly did not want to go through with it. On June 29, 1994, Charles and Dimbleby made a joint television appearance, in an attempt to "paint a more human and appealing portrait of the Prince of Wales"—an attempt which "appeared to backfire", in the words of one newspaper:

"...In the course of a two-and-a-half-hour television documentary, the heir to the British throne admitted that he had committed adultery.

"Three-quarters of the way through the largely sympathetic portrayal, the Prince, sitting a little stiffly on a chintz-covered sofa at his estate at Highgrove in Gloucestershire, is asked point blank if he tried to be "faithful and honorable" when he married Lady Diana Spencer in July 1981.

"Yes, absolutely," he replied.

"And you were?" pressed the questioner, Jonathan Dimbleby, a well-known British journalist.

"Yes," Prince Charles answered. Then after a slight pause he added, "Until it became irretrievably broken down, us both having tried."

The fact was, even though "Charles's side", as Diana put it, were working round the clock to rehabilitate his image, Diana was still the star of the royal show, whether anyone in the Palace liked it or not. She had realized a long time ago that if the people were going to continue to regard the monarchy as relevant to their society, the monarchy would have to begin responding to the changing times—to abandon stiffness and behave like relatable human beings in public as well as private. Yet even though she had gone into her separation from Charles determined to remain devoted to her official work as the Princess of Wales, she found that the Palace was organizing itself to diminish her relevance to the best of its ability. Diana had a keener instinct than most for the places and occasions where an official royal presence would do the most good, but after the separation, she often found that her proposed trips abroad were vetoed, for no particular reason, only for Charles to be sent along on the same trip a few weeks later. Her frustration with this game led her to announce, in early December of 1993, almost exactly one year after the start of her separation from

Charles, that she was withdrawing from public life. In the statement she made to the press, she said:

"When I started my public life 12 years ago, I understood that the media might be interested in what I did. I realized then that their attention would inevitably focus on both our private and public lives. But I was not aware of how overwhelming that attention would become; nor the extend to which it would affect both my public duties and my personal life, in a manner that has been hard to take... My first priority will continue to be our children, William and Harry, who deserve as much love, care, and attention as I am able to give, as well as an appreciation of the tradition into which they were born."

Of course, it was impossible for the most famous woman in the world to "retire from public life" in the sense of disappearing from the public eye.

Her retirement simply meant that she would no longer act as an official representative of the royal family, save on rare occasions involving her children. She continued to make speeches in support of causes she was passionate about, and she renewed her focus on providing William and Harry with experiences that would teach them compassion and expose them to real world suffering and problems in a way that would encourage them to make a positive difference when they were older. No member of the royal family, especially no heir to the throne, had ever been encouraged or permitted to interact with the world outside Buckingham Palace in the way that William and Harry were while their mother was alive. But the careers that Prince William and Prince Harry have led as adults clearly demonstrate the depth of Diana's influence. Their notion of royal duty, and appropriate public behavior, reflects Diana's understanding that the monarchy must be seen to be human and vulnerable as well as strong and uplifting.

Watching Charles's interview with Jonathan Dimbleby was a bitter experience for Diana—he had never talked to her honestly about Camilla, so it was rather galling that the first time she heard the truth from his own lips, it was at the same time as millions of other people, on a television program. But when Charles acknowledged that divorce was probably "in the future", it opened a new door for Diana, who had determined that Charles must be the one to raise "the D-word". As Andrew Morton puts it, "As far as she was concerned it was Charles who had asked her to marry him, and it was Charles who must request a divorce." The divorce of the Prince and Princess of Wales, however long anticipated and however well prepared for, would be nothing less than a constitutional crisis, and Diana was not about to place herself in the position of being blamed for triggering it. Yet as much as she longed to be finally free of her marriage, she was less sanguine about the loss of her royal status, which encompassed her official relationship with Buckingham Palace and her right to be styled "Your Royal Highness". She still had work to do—work that was sometimes only possible because royalty was a magical key that opened practically every door—and she was concerned that her effectiveness on the world stage would be diminished after the divorce. She knew she was seen by the Palace and its courtiers—the "men in grey", as Diana called them—as an unprecedented "problem", a Princess of Wales who did not have a Prince, and thus did not have a secure leash they could tug.

Her growing anxieties and frustrations with the Palace instilled in her, once more, the desire to tell her story to the public. In Andrew Morton's book she had found a safe way to express her feelings and her truth, but because her cooperation in the book's writing was still a secret, there had never yet been an official statement direct from Diana's mouth about her troubled marriage and Charles's infidelity. She had received requests from numerous high-profile journalists to be interviewed on television, including one from the BBC program Panorama that arrived around the same time as Charles was filming his documentary with Jonathan Dimbleby. But Diana was still clearing her public appearances through the Palace at the time, and the Palace had been adamantly opposed to her making any television appearances. It was thus under secret conditions that Diana agreed to be interviewed for Panorama by Martin Bashir in 1995. The program would appear in November, about five months after Charles's documentary had first aired.

Diana was quite nervous in the run up to the interview's being broadcast. She and the BBC crew had resorted to extreme measures of subterfuge in order to shoot the interview at Kensington Palace without word getting back to the Queen's press office, or indeed, anyone else at Buckingham Palace. The crew had used special miniature cameras to film the interview, and Diana had dismissed her entire staff of 12 for the day, conscious that she could trust no one. The day before the broadcast, she drove to Eton, at the request of William's headmaster, and explained to William what was going to happen, assuring him, quite inaccurately, that there would be nothing especially controversial in the interview. But in fact, Diana had already begun to worry that she had made a mistake by granting the interview. And watching it was a painful experience for William, who viewed the program alone in his headmaster's office. He discovered, for the first time, that his parents' marriage was ending because his father had been having an affair with another woman. Diana had concealed this from him up to that point, remembering all too well how painful it had been for herself and her siblings when her own parents had divorced after her mother had fallen in love with another man.

Martin Bashir's notoriously relentless style of questioning his interview subjects made Diana's interview considerably more of an ordeal for her than Charles's friendly, face-saving documentary with Jonathan Dimbleby had been for him. Bashir's questions covered, in essence, the same ground as Andrew Morton's book, but this time Diana would be speaking without an intermediary. She was understandably more diplomatic and reserved in speaking to Bashir than she had been when she was being interviewed by the go-between who had interviewed her on Morton's behalf, as is clear in the segment of the transcript reproduced below, where Bashir presses her about Charles's infidelity:

Bashir: Around 1986, again according to the biography written by Jonathan Dimbleby about your husband, he says that your husband renewed his relationship with Mrs Camilla Parker-Bowles. Were you aware of that?

Diana: Yes, I was, but I wasn't in a position to do anything about it.

Bashir: What evidence did you have that their relationship was continuing even though you were married?

Diana: Oh, a woman's instinct is a very good one.

Bashir: Is that all?

Diana: Well, I had, obviously I had knowledge of it.

Bashir: From staff?

Diana: Well, from people who minded and cared about our marriage, yes.

Bashir: What effect did that have on you?

Diana: Pretty devastating. Rampant bulimia, if you can have rampant bulimia, and just a feeling of being no good at anything and being useless and hopeless and failed in every direction.

Bashir: And with a husband who was having a relationship with somebody else?

Diana: With a husband who loved someone else, yes.

Bashir: You really thought that?

Diana: Uh, uh. I didn't think that, I knew it.

Bashir: How did you know it?

Diana: By the change of behavioural pattern in my husband; for all sorts of reasons that a woman's instinct produces; you just know. It was already difficult, but it became increasingly difficult.

Bashir: In the practical sense, how did it become difficult?

Diana: Well, people were - when I say people I mean friends, on my husband's side - were indicating that I was again unstable, sick, and should be put in a home of some sort in order to get better. I was almost an embarrassment.

Bashir: Do you think he really thought that?

Diana: Well, there's no better way to dismantle a personality than to isolate it.

Bashir: So you were isolated?

Diana: Uh, uh, very much so.

Bashir: Do you think Mrs Parker-Bowles was a factor in the breakdown of your marriage?

Diana: Well, there were three of us in this marriage, so it was a bit crowded.

Not unexpectedly, Bashir also questioned Diana about Andrew Morton's book and her involvement in its writing. While Diana did not go so far as to admit that she had recorded hours of interview material for Morton to use, she acknowledged that she had given permission to her closest friends and family to speak to Morton. By admitting as much, she effectively endorsed everything he had written. Until her death, when Morton revealed the existence of those interviews, *Diana: Her True Story* was referred to as a "semi-authorized" biography.

Bashir: The Queen described 1992 as her 'annus horribilis', and it was in that year that Andrew Morton's book about you was published. Did you ever meet Andrew Morton or personally help him with the book?

Diana: I never met him, no.

Bashir: Did you ever personally assist him with the writing of his book?

Diana: A lot of people saw the distress that my life was in, and they felt it was a supportive thing to help in the way that they did.

Bashir: Did you allow your friends, your close friends, to speak to Andrew Morton?

Diana: Yes, I did. Yes, I did.

Bashir: Why?

Diana: I was at the end of my tether. I was desperate. I think I was so fed up with being seen as someone who was a basket-case, because I am a very strong person and I know that causes complications in the system that I live in.

Bashir: How would a book change that?

Diana: I don't know. Maybe people have a better understanding, maybe there's a lot of women out there who suffer on the same level but in a different environment, who are unable to stand up for themselves because their self-esteem is cut into two. I don't know.

Bashir: What effect do you think the book had on your husband and the Royal Family?

Diana: I think they were shocked and horrified and very disappointed.

Bashir: Can you understand why?

Diana: I think Mr Dimbleby's book was a shock to a lot of people and disappointment as well.

Bashir: What effect did Andrew Morton's book have on your relationship with the Prince of Wales?

Diana: Well, what had been hidden - or rather what we thought had been hidden - then became out in the open and was spoken about on a daily basis, and the pressure was for us to sort ourselves out in some way. Were we going to stay together or were we going to separate? And the word separation and divorce kept coming up in the media on a daily basis.

Bashir: What happened after the book was published?

Diana: Well, we struggled along. We did our engagements together. And in our private life it was obviously turbulent.

Bashir: Did things come to a head?

Diana: Yes, slowly, yes. My husband and I, we discussed it very calmly.

If Charles's interview with Dimbleby had opened the door for Diana to discuss divorce with him, Diana's interview with Bashir made it clear to the Queen that the divorce must take place before any more damage was done to the monarchy by the feuding between the couple. On February 28, 1996, which Diana described as "the saddest day of my life", the uncontested divorce was finalized and announced—not by the Palace, but by Diana herself, who pre-empted the Queen's press secretary without notice or permission. Diana's statement read: "The Princess of Wales has agreed to Prince Charles's request for a divorce. The Princess will continue to be involved in all decisions relating to the children and will remain at Kensington Palace, with offices in St James's Palace. The Princess of Wales will retain the title and be known as Diana, Princess of Wales."

In fact, no final agreement on Diana's titles and styles had been decided upon by the Queen, and she was irritated by the statement, as was Charles, who had not agreed that her offices would remain at St. James's. Six weeks later, the Palace announced the terms of the divorce settlement. Diana received all she had asked for—unimpeded access to her children (the Queen herself had assured Diana that she would never take William and Harry away from her), a lump sum alimony payment of £17 million, and her offices at St. James's. She would still be considered a member of the royal family, and would continue to be known as the Princess of Wales. But she would no longer be styled "Her Royal Highness". The only difference this made, practically speaking, was that Diana would be obligated to curtsey and give precedence to anyone who was a Royal Highness, including her own sons. Stripping her of the appellation was a spiteful and pointless move, and it was said to be one that Charles insisted on over the Queen's objections. It meant a great deal more to him than it did to Diana—but then it had also meant a great deal to the uncle Charles so resembled, the Duke of Windsor, who had been deeply embittered when his own wife, Wallis Simpson, was denied an "HRH" after their marriage. Diana thought it was absurd that she should have to curtsey to anyone other than the Queen and Prince Philip, but otherwise, was content simply to be Princess of Wales, a position which would continue to open the necessary doors for her work.

"Queen of people's hearts"

Now a single woman—the first single Princess of Wales in British history—Diana was free to "spring clean" her life. Her first priority after looking after William and Harry was to figure out ways to more effectively use her astonishing fame and popularity to do good in the world. She had attempted to emphasize in her interview with Martin Bashir that she intended to play a significant role as a humanitarian ambassador for Britain in her post-royal existence, though of course this was scarcely noted amidst the bombshells about her and Charles's infidelity towards each other. Andrew Morton writes that:

"One of the many perplexing contradictions about Diana was that while she did not value herself highly as an individual she did understand her worth on the public stage, seeing that her standing in society, both at home and abroad, gave her a unique springboard to support the causes and issues she cherished. Yet she was deeply disenchanted with the protocol, the flummery and the artifice which inevitably surrounded royalty. Her challenge was to reinvent her public persona, to discard the robes of her office whilst retaining her authority."

As part of her efforts to reinvent herself after her divorce, she shed most of the trappings of her royal existence—most of her staff, servants, chauffeurs, and even her wardrobe. At William's suggestion, Diana auctioned off the outrageously glamorous gowns she had worn as Charles's wife to raise money for AIDS research. She resigned from most of the charities on her portfolio, specifically the ones which had been assigned to her by the Palace, because the need to attend countless balls and galas took time away from researching the causes closest to her heart, such AIDS, leprosy, eating disorders, and shelters for battered women.

When Tony Blair became Prime Minister in 1997, he invited Diana to his new country retreat, Chequers, to discuss how Diana could serve Britain as an official ambassador with a humanitarian rather than a political portfolio, a person who could "pour oil on troubled waters" and facilitate communication between warring parties in various parts of the world. Inquiries had been made under the previous Prime Minister about Diana's serving in this sort of capacity, but the Palace had responded that this was the sort of work which naturally belonged to the Prince of Wales, not his divorced wife. Blair, however, saw much greater potential in Diana's abilities than the Palace did—his concern was the good of the country as a whole, rather than saving face for an increasingly unpopular monarchy. After Diana's death, Blair remarked that she "had a tremendous ability, as we saw over the landmines issue, to enter into an area that could have been one of controversy and suddenly just clarify for people what was the right thing to do. That in itself was an extraordinary attribute and I felt there were all sorts of ways that could have been harnessed and used for the good of the people."

Diana's death would coincide, most ironically, with Tony Blair's first official day in office as

Prime Minister, but there were weeks beforehand during which she was filled with excitement and a renewed sense of self worth thanks to Blair's confidence in her. "I think at last I will have someone who will know how to use me," Diana told a friend after the Chequers summit. "[Blair's] told me he wants me to go on some missions. I'd really like to go to China. I'm very good at sorting people's heads out."

Dodi Fayed

Diana was never entirely reconciled to the relationship between Charles and Camilla Parker-Bowles. On the one hand, she was long past the days when their affair excited any jealousy, and told a friend that "I wish him well"—she thought it only right that Camilla be rewarded for her decades of devotion and tact by being made a public part of Charles's life. Still, she deeply resented what she saw as the wasted years of her marriage and her youth, a waste for which Camilla had been partly responsible. Diana was still, in spite of all her growth, a vulnerable and rather emotionally starved person, and she longed for a true fairy tale romance with a good man who would cherish her, someone powerful and strong enough to cope with the baggage that dating the Princess of Wales would inevitably entail.

But she knew how desperately unlikely it was that she would ever find anything of the sort. Her most innocent friendships with men had always been splashed over the newspapers as though they were evidence of infidelity, and the rare, brief romances she had entertained with her bodyguards had been exposed—one by illegal phone surveillance, and one by her lover selling his story. Any relationship she had with a man, no matter how honest and sincere and above-board, could be made to look dirty by a salacious press, and Diana was acutely aware that the

Palace might begin to raise questions about whether it was appropriate for William and Harry to spend time with her if there was a chance of them meeting a new man in her life. Diana's former in-laws were the most powerful and feared family in the country, and if they really wanted to take her sons away from her, she would be powerless to stop them—though she probably underestimated her power to retaliate against them. Diana understood why her popularity was considered threatening by the Palace, but it was not an obsession with her, whereas it had to be one for the Queen's courtiers. Although the hideous backlash which the royal family suffered after Diana's death took all of them very much by surprise, it was not so surprising to the machinery of the monarchy, who had always feared Diana's power to rock the ship of state.

Diana's cool yet charitable attitude towards Camilla Parker-Bowles was responsible for her decision, in June of 1997, to go on holiday to St-Tropez with Mohamed al-Fayed and his family. Camilla's 50th birthday was approaching, and Charles was planning to host a party for her at Highgrove—an understated way of marking the official beginning of their public relationship. Aware that the media would take a deep interest in whatever Diana was doing at the time of the party, interpreting her activities as a commentary on her feelings about Charles and Camilla's relationship, Diana decided she could not do better than to get out of England for a bit—strangely enough, she did not wish to overshadow Camilla's moment in the sun. Mohamed al-Fayed, a wealthy Egyptian businessman who was at the time the owner of Harrods department store, had been a close friend of the Spencer family for many years. He had often remarked that he and the late Earl Spencer had been as close as brothers. Al-Fayed had issued a standing invitation for Diana and her sons to join him and his family at his villa in the South of France whenever she liked. He himself had four sons—the oldest of which was the 41-year old Hollywood producer Emad al-Fayed, known as Dodi.

Contrary to what was assumed by the media after Diana was photographed with Dodi's family in St-Tropez, she did not know him well, nor was she romantically involved with him when she decided to accept his father's invitation. In fact, Dodi did not join the family party until four days into the trip, and even then he stayed on own yacht with his then-girlfriend. In short, Diana's holiday with the al-Fayeds was not a romantic getaway, but rather one of her many attempts to find a safe getaway spot where she could take William and Harry for a little peace during the part of the summer vacation they would spend with her. No doubt she could have chosen a more anonymous spot than the South of France, a well-known retreat for the rich and famous, but unlike most people in her set, she did not own extensive properties and country retreats. She was a single mother supported by alimony—albeit on a royal scale—and it was still early days since her divorce. She hadn't had a chance to establish the sort of home she wanted, where William and Harry could spend time with her safely shielded from the glare of camera lenses. A holiday in St-Tropez in the company of one of her father's best friends was the closest Diana could come to organizing a private family vacation for the boys, and she was grateful to al-Fayed for providing the opportunity.

Despite being harassed by photographers during the trip, Diana considered her visit to St-Tropez "the best holiday of my life". She and Dodi had become good friends by the end of the visit. Though he had a reputation as a playboy and was notorious for a lifestyle of conspicuous consumption, he had known tragedy early in life due to the death of his mother, and possessed a combination of surface flightiness mingled with a deep inner sadness which made him attractive to a person like Diana, who had a keen intuition for sensing suffering in other people. These were more or less the same qualities that had made Charles attractive to her in the early days. Furthermore, Dodi passed the acid test for any man who wanted to become involved in her life: he was marvelous with William and Harry. He had even gone to the trouble of renting out a disco for two nights just so Diana and the boys could dance and be silly in private without fear of being photographed.

Dodi and Diana remained in touch after the holiday ended, a close friendship soon turned into what seemed like a promising young romance. Now that Charles and Camilla were officially a couple, Diana felt free to have a public fling of her own—the first in her life since she began dating Charles sixteen years before. Dodi's father was ecstatic about their developing relationship. He could think of nothing more desirable than that his eldest son should marry the most glamorous woman on earth. Dodi seemed to fall for Diana as quickly as his father fell for the idea of the two of them. His friends observed that he seemed more serious after he met her, as though he had determined to give up his playboy flightiness and put in the work that would be needed to make the relationship possible.

Diana's feelings about Dodi Fayed have been speculated about endlessly. Because they only began dating a few weeks before their deaths, there was only a short window of opportunity for her to confide in her friends and family, or indeed, decide for herself what her feelings were. She told one friend that, "I adore him," and that she had "never been so happy", and there is some evidence that Fayed might have been intending to propose to Diana on the night they were both killed. But after their deaths, when Mohamed al-Fayed claimed that Diana and Dodi had been on the point of getting engaged, some of Diana's friends asserted that the relationship was, for her, only a fling, and that she was growing irritated with Fayed's tendency to try and control her life. The truth cannot be known at this point; but it does seem that, whether she intended to marry him or not, Fayed provided Diana with many pleasant, carefree hours in the final weeks of her life.

The death of Diana, Princess of Wales

The last few days of Diana's life were probably the happiest she had ever known. She finally seemed to have everything she needed from life—a professional future as a humanitarian ambassador that would fulfill her lifelong desire to serve the public, an enjoyable romantic relationship with a man who was devoted to her, as much freedom from the royal establishment as she could ever expect to have, the knowledge that her sons, now 15 and 13, were growing up to be grounded, decent young men. She had her health back, and was enjoying more peace of mind than ever before in her life. Even her relationship with Prince Charles had reached a stage of comparative friendliness. In a way, for those who loved her, this made her death a little easier to bear; but it also seemed bitterly unfair that she should be snatched out of the world just when her suffering was over and she had a chance at some of the sweetness of life.

It was August 31, 1997, and Diana and Dodi were on the final day of their second holiday alone in each other's accompany; they had sailed Dodi's yacht off the coast of Sardinia, and they were scheduled to spend a night in Paris having dinner at Dodi's apartment before Diana returned to Britain to see her sons. The paparazzi had been a special nuisance throughout the trip, especially once they reached Paris, where photographers on motorcycles raced after their car and drove up dangerously close to their vehicles to get shots of the couple through the windows. Diana was irritated by their behavior, but, characteristically, she was more concerned that one of them would get into an accident and be hurt, given the recklessness of their driving. After arriving in Paris, she and Dodi retreated to the Ritz hotel to rest and get changed for dinner. There, Diana received a phone call from William. He had been asked to pose for photographs at Eton, as part of the arrangement the Palace had negotiated with the media, which stipulated that in exchange for leaving the boys in peace until they came of age, the Palace would occasionally provide official candid photographs of William and Harry going about their daily lives. Yet Harry had not been asked to take part in the photo op, and William was concerned that he would be made to feel overshadowed. Diana shared his concerns and promised him she would think about how to handle the situation. It was the last conversation William would ever have with his mother.

By the evening, the paparazzi were so thick on the ground that Dodi and Diana decided to cancel their restaurant reservations for dinner and return to the Ritz to eat at the hotel before adjourning to Dodi's apartment. There, it has since been speculated, he might have intended to propose to her. There was an engagement ring found amongst his possessions—one which Diana and Dodi had looked at together in a shop window a few weeks earlier. Dodi had also written a love poem for Diana and had it inscribed on a silver plaque, and it was waiting underneath the pillow on her side of the bed. Whether Dodi intended to propose that night or not, he was deeply anxious that they not be harassed by photographers on their return trip to his apartment. He had instructed his chauffeur, Henri Paul, to arrange for decoy vehicles to leave from the front of the hotel, while Paul whisked Dodi, Diana, and their bodyguard, Trevor Rees-

Jones, away via the service entrance at the back of the hotel.

Paul deployed the decoy cars successfully, but some photographers spotted the Mercedes parked by the service entrance, and set off in pursuit. Paul, who was high on drugs and heavily intoxicated—his blood alcohol level was three times the limit legal for driving—took off at high speed. At 12:24 am, he drove into an underpass tunnel, going an estimated 85-95 miles per hour, where he lost control of the vehicle and collided with a concrete pillar. Both Henri Paul and Dodi Fayed were killed instantly. Trevor Rees-Jones, who was the only person in the Mercedes wearing a seat belt, was badly injured, though he regained consciousness after two weeks.

Diana suffered severe crush injuries to her head and chest, and she was alive for approximately twenty minutes after the first medical professionals on the scene began to treat her, although she was not declared dead until 4 am. Her mother later assured the public that, "I know the extent of her injuries and I promise everyone that she knew nothing. She did not suffer at all." The entire royal family, including William and Harry, were at Balmoral. The Queen, Prince Philip, and Charles were awakened in the middle of the night and informed that Diana had been in a car crash and was severely injured; shortly afterwards, they learned from the radio that she was dead. Charles stayed up for the rest of the night, but he waited until morning to tell his sons what had happened to their mother. He traveled on a royal jet to return Diana's body to England, and after she had been dressed and made presentable in clothing brought to the airport by her devoted butler, Paul Burrell, her closest family members and staff were allowed to see her and make their private farewells. Prince Charles remained alone in the room with his ex-wife and the mother of his children for half an hour, and when he came out again, it was clear that he had been crying.

Later that morning, Tony Blair gave an official statement which captured the spirit of universal mourning which had engulfed Britain, and most of the rest of the world as well:

"I feel like everyone else in this country today. I am utterly devastated. Our thoughts and prayers are with Princess Diana's family, particularly her two sons. Our heart goes out to them... We are today a nation in a state of shock, in mourning, in grief that is so deeply painful for us.

"She was a wonderful and a warm human being, although her own life was often sadly touched by tragedy. She touched the lives of so many others in Britain and throughout the world with joy and with comfort. How many times shall we remember her in how many different ways -

with the sick, the dying, with children, with the needy?

"With just a look or a gesture that spoke so much more than words, she would reveal to all of us the depth of her compassion and her humanity.

"We know how difficult things were for her from time to time. I am sure we can only guess that. But people everywhere, not just here in Britain, kept faith with Princess Diana."

The public outpouring of grief which Diana's death provoked was a phenomenon practically without precedent in modern times. The gates outside the palace were blanketed with flowers, cards, stuffed animals, and other tributes from people who felt that they had lost someone important in their lives. The deaths of popular celebrities generally trigger displays of mourning from the public that admired them, but the worldwide reaction to Diana's death was on a different scale—dubbed "the Diana phenomenon", it was almost religious in nature. People sobbed in public and hugged strangers in the streets; counselors and therapists were besieged by patients who found that Diana's death had triggered long-buried feelings about grief and loss in their own life. It was as if the compassion which had driven her career was being mirrored back at her by every person who had ever read her biography, watched her on television, or even purchased a magazine with her face on the cover. As Tony Blair famously said at the end of his speech:

"They liked her, they loved her, they regarded her as one of the people. She was the People's Princess and that is how she will stay, how she will remain in our hearts and our memories forever."

Other great books by Michael W. Simmons on Kindle, paperback and audio:

Elizabeth I: Legendary Queen Of England

Alexander Hamilton: First Architect Of The American Government

William Shakespeare: An Intimate Look Into The Life Of The Most Brilliant Writer In The History Of The English Language

Thomas Edison: American Inventor

Catherine the Great: Last Empress of Russia

Romanov: The Last Tsarist Dynasty

Peter the Great: Autocrat and Reformer

The Rothschilds: The Dynasty and the Legacy

Queen Victoria: Icon of an Era

Six Wives: The Women Who Married, Lived, and Died for Henry VIII

John D. Rockefeller: The Wealthiest Man in American History

Princess to Queen: The Early Years of Queen Elizabeth II

Further Reading

Diana, In Her Own Words, Andrew Morton

Speeches given by Diana, Princess of Wales, on AIDS and Landmines

http://www.theroyalforums.com/forums/f38/dianas-speeches-and-quotes-1353.html

"How Diana Broke the Queen's Heart"

http://www.dailymail.co.uk/news/article-3479619/How-Diana-broke-Queen-s-heart-Based-new-interviews-Majesty-s-inner-circle-truth-explosive-battle-wills-revealed-one-definitive-portrait.html

Transcript of BBC Panorama interview with Martin Bashir

http://www.bbc.co.uk/news/special/politics97/diana/panorama.html

"Prince Charles Admits to Infidelity"

http://www.nytimes.com/1994/06/30/world/prince-charles-in-tv-documentary-admits-to-infidelity.html

Obituary of Diana, Princess of Wales

http://www.telegraph.co.uk/news/obituaries/royalty-obituaries/1542104/Diana-Princess-of-Wales.html

Made in the USA
Monee, IL
07 December 2020